# FAITH
## AT
# WORK

# FAITH
## AT
# WORK

*Overcoming the Obstacles of Being*
*Like Christ in the Workplace*

## MICHAEL A. ZIGARELLI, PH.D.

**MOODY PRESS**
CHICAGO

ISBN: 0-8024-6189-1

1 3 5 7 9 10 8 6 4 2

*Printed in the United States of America*

*To my students, both past and present,
who faithfully endeavor to apply the
Beatitudes in the workplace.
You'll encounter many obstacles to this
pursuit throughout your career.
But the better you know these obstacles,
the better equipped you'll be to overcome them—
and to more successfully live your
Faith at Work.*

# CONTENTS

# Introduction

# WHAT MATTERS
# *MOST* IN YOUR JOB

*Now when he saw the crowds, he went
up on a mountainside and sat down.
. . . and he began to teach them.*
MATTHEW 5:1–2

If you're like I am, you work for a living. It's not always fun, it's not always meaningful, but most months it pays the bills.

Let me ask you to take two minutes and think about this job of yours. Think about the tasks involved, the people with whom you typically associate, the work environment, the product or service you provide. Think about what you like and don't like about it. And think about what you're doing in your work life that matters the most.

That last one is kind of tricky. Many of us can rattle off our daily routine to anyone who asks. And we could talk for days about what we enjoy at work and (especially) what can be improved. Identifying what *really matters* in our work—what has lasting significance—is another question, though. A critically important question.

To better answer it, come at this from another an-

gle. This approach has been helpful to a countless
number of my undergraduate and MBA students.
Fast-forward the tape of your work life to a few years
down the road. You're now retiring. There's a dinner
to honor you and all the others in your cohort who
have earned the gold watch (or pewter plaque, de-
pending on the generosity of your employer). Look
around the room. Who's there? Who is speaking with
whom? What's the mood in the place? Do people
seem to be enjoying themselves? From across the
room, a co-worker glances over at you and whispers
to a friend. The friend responds with a nod, eye contact, and a casual wave. A lot of people are talking
about you tonight because this is your night. What are
they saying?

The time comes for the obligatory short speeches
commemorating, thanking—sometimes roasting—
the retirees. One by one, employees come to the microphone to share stories and raise a glass. Some
stories are funny, some are touching, some seem
merely polite. Obviously, there wasn't much to say
about *that* person. Then up steps the person slated
to say a few words about you, your career, your con-
tribution—about all you've meant to the organization. What will this person say? What is it about you
that will be remembered as significant? What is it
about all of those years—about all of that effort—that
this person thinks *really mattered?*

If you would, let that set in for a second. Don't sell
yourself short by rushing through this exercise.
What's being spotlighted in this short speech? Ac-
complishments? Securing clients? Work ethic? Your
personality? What will stand out when others reflect

on the job to which you gave your life?

Now take this scene one last step. Imagine for a moment that the person at the podium is not your co-worker, but Jesus Christ Himself. You didn't know He had a ticket to this shindig, but there He is, scars and all. He even managed to somehow get around the jacket-only requirement.

Unlike the other speakers, though, He elects to sit down with the microphone—and right next to you. The room falls strangely silent—more quiet than it was for the others—as He says your name. A smile comes to His face, a smile of caring, a smile of friendship. He says your name again. "I'm going to tell you good folks what this employee did at work all of these years that *really mattered,*" He begins.

You listen in awe at what's chronicled over the next few minutes. Everyone in the room is captivated by just how different this speech is from all the others. What Jesus emphasizes as important is quite unlike what was emphasized by the other speakers. Had you only known Jesus' opinion on what your goals should be on the job . . . had you only been able to see what was preventing you from pursuing those goals . . . had you only heard His words decades ago . . .

What matters most in the Christian's work life is not what matters to the world. It's not the size of the paycheck, the impressiveness of the business card, the prestige, or the number of battles won. It's not even your productivity or the quality of your work, although hard work is certainly a worthy pursuit. Instead, when it comes to your job, *what matters most to the Man with the microphone is the extent to which you were Christlike from 9 to 5.*

---

*When it comes to your job, what matters most to God is the extent to which you were Christlike from 9 to 5.*

---

Stop the presses! This is a revelation, right?

Hardly. Most of us Christians know this implicitly. We hear it pretty regularly from the pulpit. Problem is, our thinking gets transformed from Sunday to Monday. Invisible but powerful workplace realities create obstacles to Christlikeness on the job. Some are work environment realities, some are innate to our nature, but all of them relegate God's priorities to the backseat. By Tuesday, they may fade from the rearview mirror altogether.

From what I've seen, that's a source of continuing frustration for many Christians. We struggle with it. We feel guilty about it. We may even recommit for a while to doing things differently on the job. Somehow, though, many of us backslide into this traditional mind-set about how we should think and act in the workplace. Actually, it's more accurate to say that several barriers bulldoze us back down the hill. We don't stand a chance of permanent progress unless we can sidestep the heavy equipment along the way.

Perhaps you, too, have had some personal experience with this. Perhaps you've made some effort to apply your faith in the workplace, only to be repeatedly discouraged by the results. Perhaps you've even reached the point of concluding that real, enduring change is hopeless for you. *It's not.* It's just a matter of seeing more clearly—maybe for the first time in your life—the many obstacles that have prevented you from modeling Christ on a daily basis. And then it's a matter of cooperating with God to defeat them.

What are these obstacles and how can we finally overcome them? *Faith at Work* is a project dedicated to answering these questions. Tapping the insights of the Beatitudes, of the best available workplace research, and of several Christians who have struggled with these tensions in their own lives, this book offers you some ideas about how to avoid eight primary stumbling blocks to consistently emulating Christ in the workplace. As noted in the table of contents, I've labeled these "Your Personal Golden Calf," "Monday Mourning," "The 'Meekness Is Weakness' Myth," "A 'Fight for Your Rights' Mentality," "Compassion Fatigue," "Ingratitude," "Being an 'Eye for an Eye' Guy," and "People-Pleasing."

What's keeping you from being more Christlike in your job and in your career? What are the barriers that have always stood in your way? And how can you overcome them to pursue what *really matters* at work? These are questions worth exploring long before your retirement dinner.

Obstacle 1

# YOUR PERSONAL GOLDEN CALF

*Blessed are the poor in spirit,*
*for theirs is the kingdom of heaven.*
MATTHEW 5:3

It's a story of faith and hypocrisy.

Four-year-old Tom walked solemnly to his father's casket. It wasn't fair. It didn't make sense. Why would God take his daddy? And of all times, why on Christmas Eve?

The boy reached into the casket to shake his father. He was about to shout, "Daddy! Please wake up!" But in that instant his family pulled him away.[1] Even the mortician was moved by the scene.

His father's passing changed Tom's life forever, as did his mother's subsequent decision to give up Tom for adoption. Over the next few years, Tom and his younger brother, James, were shuttled in and out of Catholic orphanages because their mother was too poor to raise them. There, Tom learned a little more about God but still remained confused about Him.

As the years rolled by, it became apparent that Tom wasn't going to be an academic superstar. He did, however, earn quite a reputation in the orphanage for his efficiency. In fact, quickness became his trademark. He could iron a pile of laundry faster than anyone, and with the next heap, he'd try to beat his own record. This distinction made Tom feel smart. It gave him a niche, a claim to fame, a place of relevance in a world where everyone else seemed to have so much more.

Tom was eventually adopted, and although it felt great to be out of the orphanage, he was self-conscious about being poor. God was still part of his life, but as Tom matured, his thoughts tended to center more on wealth and popularity. At the time, he couldn't do much about the wealth, but he could work on the popularity. In high school, he worked on it to the point of obsession as he sought to excel in sports and to date only the best-looking girls.

After high school, Tom wanted to attend college to study architecture, but—same story as always—no money. So he tried to build a college fund by starting a small business selling pizzas. At first, like any eager entrepreneur, Tom worked incessantly, regularly putting in one-hundred-hour workweeks. It was his penchant for quickness, though, that evolved into the marketing strategy that paid off big time: pizza delivered in thirty minutes or less.

Decades later, Domino's Pizza had made Tom Monaghan a billionaire. And as the money poured in through the 1970s and 1980s, Tom lived out his dreams: expensive cars, $12,000 wristwatches, $7,000 vases, helicopters, planes, and yachts—there was nothing the once-impoverished orphan denied himself. He built a lavish, 2,500-acre golf course retreat, worked in a $2 million office, and broke ground on a 20,000-square-foot home. He even bought the beloved ball team of his youth, the Detroit Tigers, for a svelte $53 million. Now this was the American dream, a real rags-to-riches story.

Problem is, though, one who's living this sort of American dream does not easily fit through the eye of a needle. And Tom Monaghan knew it. He had risen to be the world's pizza delivery king, while only paying lip service to the King who had delivered him. Sure, he'd given plenty to charities and to the church. He was even a nationally renowned champion of pro-life causes. Tom had seemingly done many good things externally, but on the inside, he had never surrendered his life to God. His heart was hard and his extravagant living reflected that—until, that is, C. S. Lewis performed some CPR.

When he read about pride in Lewis's classic, *Mere Christianity,* Monaghan's eyes were opened, literally as well as figuratively. The fifty-something CEO lay in bed all night taking inventory of his life, wrestling with the icy awareness that his prodigal lifestyle had been "to get attention, to have people notice me."[2] Regardless of his charitable works, Tom's god wasn't really the God of Jesus Christ. No, Tom's god was *Tom*—his reputation and his empire.

The insight was as shocking as his moment at the casket. "I realized that I had more pride than any person I know," says Tom of his revelation. "I'm the biggest hypocrite there is."[3]

———

It's a story about a low-level employee in Tom Monaghan's company who also got caught up in pleasing the crowd.

Craig was a nineteen-year-old delivery boy. This wasn't his first job, and it certainly wasn't his career of choice. He really wanted to attend seminary someday, or at least do something that made a difference in this world. But right now, he just needed the money.

The work environment wasn't bad. The guys there were pretty cool. And since Craig had to be with these people each day, he wanted to fit in.

It was sort of a strange work culture, though. His co-workers would do things like put Ex-Lax into the manager's coffeepot just for a laugh. They would plug the office computer into The Clapper and then howl when later that day the machine mysteriously shut off—taking all of the boss's work with it. During slower times of the day, they'd hang out, gossiping and complaining. On deliveries, they'd visit friends on the way back to the restaurant. Deep down, it didn't seem right to Craig. In fact, when he thought about it in the pews each Sunday, it seemed a bit offensive. But what was he going to do? It wasn't his responsibility to set his friends straight, he concluded, so he stopped worrying about it.

Years later, Craig was still driving for Domino's. Except a few things had changed. Now Craig was the one spiking the coffee. Now Craig was taking his sweet time on the road at company expense. Now Craig was showing rookies how to do less work without getting caught. The change just sort of happened overnight. He still sat attentively in church, but his Sunday thoughts no longer included his Monday behavior.

---

It's a story of God's high priest run amok.

There he stood, liberated from the chains of Egypt, his footprints still fresh on the floor of the Red Sea. There he stood, called to lead the people to a life of piety and worship. Moses' brother Aaron was Israel's inaugural pastor, and Moses charged him to maintain control while he ascended Mount Sinai.

But there Aaron stood, gold dust on his hands, mouth agape at the sight of a brother who most assumed had perished on the mountainside. If Aaron's face weren't so red from being near the furnace, it surely would have been red from embarrassment.

His words to Moses are striking and worth memorizing: "I told them [the Israelites], 'Whoever has any gold jewelry, take it off.' Then they gave me the gold, and I threw it into the fire, and out came this calf" (Exodus 32:24).

Voila! Just like that! An extraordinary process if ever there was one. I threw in a few ingredients and miraculously out came *this!*

It wasn't a total lie, but Aaron's response certainly was intended to mask the truth and to shift the blame. We know what really happened from several verses earlier: "He [Aaron] took what they handed him and made it into an idol cast in the shape of a calf, fashioning it with a tool" (Exodus 32:4). Aaron built the thing. There's no way around it. Rather than do God's work, he succumbed to the will of those around him. He was more concerned about what his peers thought than what God thought. And to top it off, once his sin was exposed, he all but denied responsibility for it. Out of the fire came this calf! Don't ask me how it happened. I'm just as amazed as you are.[4]

## THE GOLDEN CALF IN OUR WORKPLACE

What little difference three thousand years can make! Consider the modern workplace. To whom or to what do we bow down when we are amidst the crowd? What guides the many decisions that we make each workday? What determines how hard we work? Who makes the rules for how we interact with co-workers and customers? Overall, what is it that dictates our attitude and behavior on the job?

For some people, money, power, and stature are primary motivators. Climbing the ladder and earning a good living are paramount. For some people, fitting in and being well liked are most important. Popularity, social acceptance, and respect are the answers to the above questions. Some see work as a necessary evil and are preoccupied with doing the minimum that's required. They're just going through the motions till quitting time, motivated by nothing more than keeping their jobs and drawing a paycheck.

Indeed, there are many other workplace motivators, and if some of yours haven't been mentioned, mentally tack them on. But then step back and analyze what's really going on here. When we think about our life at work, where is God? Is He still in church? Does He get checked at the company door when we walk in? Is He in a box that we take out only in time of need or crisis?

More to the point, for the Christian in the workplace, *why isn't "God" the answer to each of the job-related questions listed above?* I'd suggest there are two basic reasons for this—one for the nominal believer and one for the more mature believer.

First off, many casual Christians are simply unfamiliar with the fact that God wants to be at the center of everything we do in the workplace. They haven't been taught by anyone that there's more to Christianity than the Golden Rule. They haven't heard that God has a plan for our daily work and that He has written down principles to guide us in our jobs and careers. For many Christians, this is brand-new information.

But what about those of us who are familiar with this teaching? Why do we more learned believers persist in relegating God to the back burner on our jobs? The responses of many of the adult Christian students I have had the pleasure of teaching suggest that the answer is an ancient one. To paraphrase, many say things like "I don't really know what's happened. I tried really hard to live my faith at work, especially in my young and idealistic days, but I guess the workplace changes you. It conforms you. It makes you adopt the rules by which everyone else plays."

Read the comment again. Don't miss the implicit message. Without knowing it, they are basically responding as Aaron did. "I threw myself into the fire of the workplace and out came *these new priorities!*" It just happened.

Some of my other Christian students have placed the blame not on corporate culture, but on their bosses. Their perspective can be summarized as follows: "You have to look out for number one today. I didn't always think that, but after getting burned a few times, I now know better. Higher-ups are always asking for more, always looking for ways to squeeze more work out of you for the same pay. Well, I just give them what they're paying for."

I threw myself into the fire of the workplace and out came this preoccupation with my rights!

Similarly, a sizable percentage of Christian managers I've counseled point toward their professional training and their career aspirations as the culprits for their workplace attitudes. "The approach they teach us in business school is persuasive," they say. "We're running a business here, not a charity. I'd like to give my people more, but in a world of limited budgets and global competition, we have to treat people as just another 'factor of production.' This is in the best interest of the shareholder, the owner of this company. Besides, if word gets out that your values get in the way of your decision-making process, it's instant career cul-de-sac."

I threw myself into the fire of business school and out came this career-focused, bottom-line-oriented manager!

For Tom Monaghan, possessions and popularity were the motivators, even though deep down he knew better. For Craig, a delivery boy with seminary aspirations, it was the desire to be part of the gang that ultimately reshaped his perspective. The common denominator through all of this, though, is that we Christians—at times deliberately, at times unwittingly—too often abdicate responsibility for our workplace behavior. Aaron's words to Moses reverberate throughout the ages. "It's not really my fault," many of us would say if pressed for an explanation. "This golden calf of mine—this fixation on money, success, personal reputation, individual rights—seemingly came out of nowhere. Before I knew what was going on, there it was!"

*A golden calf can easily become the number one obstacle to Christlikeness at work.*

That may be true, but it's also ironic. These golden calves of ours exist because we think they will make us happy. We think that more money, more respect, a bigger office, a new title, a shorter workday will bring us closer to lasting satisfaction on the job. It might even give our work some greater level of meaningfulness. However, the irony for the Christian is that pursuing those things can ultimately become the number one *obstacle* to finding genuine, long-term fulfillment and purpose in our jobs. That is, they can actually *prevent* us from doing that which really matters to God—modeling Christ at work—because they act as a substitute for a God-centered life.

By contrast, a New Testament approach to consistent Christlikeness at work begins by first identifying and slaying your personal golden calf—by pinpointing and dispensing with those things that typically guide your behavior—and then replacing them with God.

## THE STARTING POINT FOR CHRISTLIKENESS AT WORK

It's a story of a man on a mountain far from Sinai. His appearance was quite ordinary. His oratory was anything but.

"Now when he saw the crowds, he went up on a mountainside and sat down. His disciples came to him, and he began to teach them, saying: 'Blessed are the poor in spirit, for theirs is the kingdom of heaven'" (Matthew 5:1–3).

Why did Jesus begin His sermon this way? Quite simply, because being poor in spirit is the beginning—the beginning of a right relationship with God, the beginning of a right relationship with one's neighbor, the beginning of an authentic Christian life. It is the beginning of our ability to live the profound teachings of the Sermon on the Mount—and as we unpack the words, we'll see that it is the beginning of a more effective witness in the workplace.

Many are confused by the term *poor in spirit*, but in reality, it's a teaching with which most of us are familiar. To be poor in spirit simply means to be humble before God, to accept God's rules, God's standards, and God's plan for our lives. It is to put our will—our spirit—second and to put God's will first.

The instruction is relatively easy to understand. It's a teaching that tells us to slay the golden calf of doing things our own way and to turn toward the One who knows the better path for our lives. But ever since an infamous couple ate from the tree in the center of the Garden of Eden, people have rebelled against the teaching. We see, for example, the resistance in the lust of King David, a man who had been given everything but still desired a married Bathsheba. We see it in the self-righteousness of Jonah as he bolted rather than help to save pagans. We see it in the materialism of a rich young man who rejected the Messiah's message that he sell all he had. We see it in the greed of Judas as he sold out the Savior for silver.

Our challenge is to do things differently. This is the calling of the very first beatitude and, as we'll see, it's echoed in the others. As Christians, we are to turn from the dubious tradition of self-sufficiency and do what may be very unnatural: to let God lead us—in all that we think and do—twenty-four hours a day, seven days a week.

## APPLYING THE PRINCIPLE IN THE WORKPLACE

When these principles are words on a page, the teaching is straightforward. Think for a moment, though, about just how radical the instruction is when applied to your work life. As a guiding workplace principle, *poor in spirit* means that God's the real Boss. He's the One for whom you primarily work. He's the One you should aim to please in every task you undertake and in every interaction with people. The implications are enormous and a bit overwhelming. This first beatitude implies that you should work to your potential even though you might be underpaid, passed over for a promotion, or exploited by whoever makes the schedule. It means that no matter how busy you are, you put your family before your career. It means not worrying about what your coworkers think of you. And it means forgiving that infuriating co-worker who seems like the poster child for original sin.

For the grocery clerk, it means standing behind the checkout counter on the eve of Thanksgiving with a smile and treating every customer with respect—even the ones who berate you because the line stretches into aisle seven. For high-tech folks, it means to resist the daily temptation to visit the Internet's red-light district. For the manager, it means to put people before profits, to advertise with integrity, to be sensitive to the needs of your subordinates, and to act as a steward, not an owner, of the financial capital with which God has entrusted you. For the over-worked secretary, it means to answer that one-thousandth call of the day with the same enthusiasm you expressed when you answered the first. For the person gifted in building relationships, it may mean using that gift to verbally and diplomatically spread the gospel, cubicle by cubicle.

Why? Because when you are poor in spirit, you no longer work for some company; you no longer work for a paycheck, for the benefits, for the promotion, or for the acclaim; and you no longer work for a fore-man, a supervisor, the CEO, the shareholders, or any other person. To be poor in spirit on the job means that, first and foremost, you work for the One who created your ability to work and you seek to honor Him in everything you do.

---

*To be poor in spirit on the job means that, first and foremost, you work for the One who created your ability to work.*

---

*It is possible.* And it can happen today if you are willing to make a deliberate decision to slay what-ever golden calf may have taken up residence in your work life and to then replace that idol with God. This

is the path of workplace wisdom. And when we finally muster the courage to set foot on it—when we in
faith decide to trust and depend on God's guidance
for our workplace attitudes and behavior—we will
reap the benefits Jesus promised for the poor in spirit: "Theirs is the kingdom of heaven."

## AN ADDED BONUS: MORE PURPOSE AND FULFILLMENT IN YOUR JOB

Indeed, this is a promise of the afterlife, but it is a
promise for this life as well. The "kingdom of heaven"
is an *experience* that has been "near" since the arrival
of Jesus (Matthew 3:2; 4:17; 12:28): an earthly experience, as Paul says, of "righteousness, peace and joy
in the Holy Spirit" (Romans 14:17). It is a promise for
today, to improve the quality of our relationships and
our lives generally.

And in a workplace context, it gives every job more
meaning, since all work that is performed to honor
God is meaningful work. This applies all the way
down to the most mundane or seemingly irrelevant
tasks you have. Performing them to please God ele-
vates the tasks to a significance they never would
have had otherwise.

What we're talking about, then, is a new mind-
set—one with the power to give you a sense of purpose on the job, perhaps for the first time in your life.
It is a mind-set that gives you a cause at work: to glorify God by your effort and your attitude. And no
cause could be more noble!

Let me be even more specific. That pointless meeting you have to attend? Contribute to your potential
to please your real Boss. That indecisive customer

who's holding up the line? Treat her with patience and dignity because that's what Jesus would do. That employee of yours who's in serious need of a raise to support his growing family? Find a way to meet his needs.

---

*This new mind-set gives you the noblest cause of all on the job: to glorify God by your effort and your attitude.*

---

It's a remarkable feeling when we hear God's "Well done!" on the job. It's a feeling of real purpose and accomplishment. And when we hear it on a consistent basis, we encounter a level of job satisfaction beyond anything we've ever experienced.

Working as if working for God allows us to access "the kingdom of heaven" here on earth. It yields an inner peace and joy far exceeding that which comes from honoring any golden calf.

## SLAYING THE CALF AT DOMINO'S

Tom Monaghan learned that lesson. "None of these things I've bought, and I mean none of them, have ever really made me happy," he said in reflection. "So anything I've got that gives me pleasure only for selfish reasons I'm selling."[5] Thus began in the early 1990s what the *Wall Street Journal* would later call "an extraordinary renunciation of material assets."[6] Monaghan disposed of the helicopter, the yacht, the plane, the radio stations, the resort, and even the Detroit Tigers, earmarking most of the proceeds for the church. And in 1998, he sold his company, further accelerating the transformation from executive to philanthropist—from rich in pride to poor in spirit. From living for others' "Well done!" to living for God's "Well done!"

Tom's former employee Craig learned the lesson too. A poignant sermon on Colossians 3:23 ("Whatever you do, work at it with all your heart, as working for the Lord, not for men") provided the stimulus for him to become more poor in spirit and to devote his work life to honoring God. Sure, he still struggles in the face of peer pressure. He still struggles with the temptation to be popular at the expense of principle. He still struggles when he has an opportunity to be lazy. But his successes are starting to outnumber his failures because his life at work is now premised on a radically different assumption: the assumption that God is his Boss, that God is in charge. Not only has that given him a sense of purpose in making and delivering pizza, it's made him happier in his work than he's ever been. And it all began when he chose to slay his golden calves of people-pleasing and minimal effort.

A guy from Chicago knows something about this lesson as well . . .

It's a story of a children's film producer who refused to sell out. But his videos sure did.

In 1991, Phil Vischer had a big idea. He wanted to produce a Christian alternative to the secular entertainment that dominates Saturday morning television. He wanted to create something that would teach

kids values without sacrificing fun. Even more ambi-
tiously, he wanted to help turn around a dying culture. If that didn't work, though, he at least wanted to
provide his own kids with an animated, values-based
program.

One problem. With almost no budget, Phil was se-
verely limited in what he could do using computer
animation. Fancy special effects were definitely out.
Elaborate characters would break the bank too. Even
characters with arms, legs, clothes, or hair were too
expensive! What possibly was left?

Talking vegetables.

Phil and his partner, college buddy Mike Nawrocki,
created a twelve-second clip of Larry the Cucumber
bouncing around on a counter. Then they sought
funding to produce a full-blown video. No takers. But
it couldn't have come as a complete shock that no
video distributor would underwrite the venture. After all, these weren't just talking vegetables; these
were *religious* talking vegetables! Big ideas don't get
much more bizarre than this.

But Phil's family and friends had faith in the project. His parents took out a second mortgage, his sister loaned him her son's college fund, and a couple
from Phil's church invested their retirement savings.
With this capital in hand, in July 1993 Phil founded
Big Idea Productions out of the spare bedroom in his
home and began to market a thirty-minute "Veggie
Tales" video in Christian magazines. Unfortunately,
by Christmas, he had received only about five hundred orders, putting him well short of black ink.

A break came in 1994 when Word Music, part of
Word Publishing, agreed to distribute Veggie Tales to

Christian bookstores. The Veggies got rave reviews, but sales were still disappointing. Later that year, however, came an even more enticing offer: the opportunity to place his loquacious legumes in every Wal-Mart in America. Larry had the potential to take the country by storm and make Phil an overnight millionaire. The only catch was that to close the deal, Phil had to delete both God and the Bible from his stories.

The situation defined the word *dilemma*. Phil's response defined the word *principled*.

"We were still starving then," says Phil, "so that was very tempting. But how can we teach God's truth and edit out God?"[7] Big Idea couldn't, so they didn't. The company stayed its course, focusing on its lofty mission to "promote biblical values and encourage spiritual growth."[8]

In 1995, word-of-mouth advertising pushed video sales to 130,000. So the larger distributors came back with a revised offer: "We don't mind the theism," they said, "but could you take the Bible verse off the end?"

"No deal," said Phil. "Our teaching has a biblical base and we don't want to cut that off."

Sales continued to spiral upward over the next two years. Big Idea surpassed the 750,000 mark in 1996 and distributed its two millionth video well before the end of 1997. Back came the big guys, but this time they were ready to do business on Phil's terms. "We want them just as they are," the video distributors said of the Veggies. "How soon can we get them?"[9]

Currently Larry and his pal Bob the Tomato are available not only in Christian bookstores but, when they're not out of stock, also adorn the shelves of re-

tailers like Kmart, Wal-Mart, Target, Musicland, Eck-
erd Drugs, and Kroger. Big Idea Productions sells
hundreds of thousands of videos *every month*, not to
mention Veggie dolls, T-shirts, and an array of other
products. Pastors are wearing VeggieTales ties to the
pulpit, and Christian college students are having Veggie
Tales parties on campuses nationwide. "Sunday morning values and Saturday morning fun" is sweeping the
culture because an unapologetic Christian remained
poor in spirit, refusing to bow before a golden calf of
fame, riches, or worldly success.

*And so can you.* In your workplace, you may feel
the pressure of Aaron, but you are always called by
the words of Christ: "Blessed are the poor in spirit."

Adopting this mind-set is a choice that the Christian needs to make on a regular basis. It's not a one-
time commitment we make tearfully as we walk the
aisle at a Billy Graham crusade. It's not something we
do only when we read a book on the subject. Rather,
to faithfully live the Christian life—especially in the
secular workplace—is to struggle on an almost daily
basis to trust God and to slay the golden calves that
are everywhere. Each time one rears its ugly head, we
have to cut it off.

If that doesn't sound like a particularly inviting
promise, look at it this way: It's not every day that you
get to fire your boss! But that's precisely what you get
to do by accepting the calling to become poor in spirit. Your life at work can reopen *today* under God's new
management.

## Self-Check

Many of us bow to golden calves in our lives but don't recognize them. Is there something, tangible or intangible, that drives your search for fulfillment at work? Are you disproportionately focused on your next promotion? Working much longer hours than your peers? Doing or saying things at work that you're really not comfortable with, just to fit in? Identify whatever golden calves exist in your work life and then slay them, replacing them with God.

### NOTES

1. Dottie Enrico, "Roots of Ambition: Childhood Experiences of Orphaned, Adopted Ignite Drive to Thrive," *USA Today*, 5 September 1997, sec. B, p. 1.

2. "The Private Penance of Tom Monaghan," *The Detroit News*, 17 November 1991, sec. A, p. 1.

3. Ibid. See also Enrico, "Roots of Ambition" sec. B, p. 1.

4. This line of thought builds on a sermon from the nineteenth-century preacher Phillips Brooks. That sermon, entitled "The Fire and the Calf," can be found in Andrew Watterson Black-wood, ed., *The Protestant Pulpit: An Anthology of Master Sermons from the Reformation to Our Own Day* (Nashville: Abingdon, 1947), 129–37.

5. "The Private Penance of Tom Monaghan," sec. A, p. 1. See also Enrico, "Roots of Ambition" sec. B, p. 1.

6. Richard Gibson, "Domino's Pizza to Be Sold for $1 Billion: Founder to Turn Attention to Philanthropy," *The Wall Street Journal Europe*, 28 September 1998, 11.

7. Steve Kloehn, "One Cool Cucumber," *Chicago Tribune,* 2 October 1998, Tempo, p. 1.

8. Big Idea Productions World Wide Web site: www.bigidea.com/company/mission.asp

9. Carolyn C. Armistead, "Vegetarian Humor . . . Bob the Tomato and Larry the Cucumber Reflect Christian Values," *Chicago Tribune,* 15 February 1998, Tempo, p. 1.

# Obstacle 2

# MONDAY MOURNING

*Blessed are those who mourn,*
*for they will be comforted.*
MATTHEW 5:4

This was *my* house. Just who did this guy think he was anyway?

A couple years back, my wife and I put our house on the market. As part of that selling process, we hosted what realtors call a "Broker's Open House," also known as an "Inspection." Several dozen realtors received invitations to tour our immaculate home. I mean the place was *pristine*—certainly no small feat with three kids under five years old! As ten o'clock rolled around, I was fully prepared for the coming masses to ooh and aah at our efforts.

That image was mercilessly shattered the instant the first wave of inspectors bolted through the door. "Hi!" I said cheerfully. I wore my finest "welcome to my humble abode" face and extended my hand. What they extended in return were grunts and a few business cards. They completely blew off the handshake. Never even looked me in the eye. Worst of all, they said *nothing* about my mastery with the vacuum!

Instead they raced through the house scribbling notes on legal pads. As one came down the stairs from my kids' bedrooms, I tried again: "There's a basement too. It's right through this door."

Nothing. No verbal response. Not a glance in my direction. And to top it off, the guy didn't even check out the basement. (Horror of horrors! Maybe I didn't have to change the kitty litter down there after all!)

As this guy whisked out my front door, I was infuriated. "*This is my house!*" I wanted to shout at the intruder. "I live here!" "I own this place!" "You're trespassing!" Then, the clincher as he sped away: "I am *not* a china cabinet!"

But at that moment, that's exactly how I felt—like a piece of furniture. What was wrong with this guy anyway?

My realtor knew. She was from the same office as Mr. Personality and had some insider information. "Don't mind him," she said in a consoling tone. "He's always like that. He just hates his job." Then she complimented me on the condition of the house.

Her analysis reminded me of some research I had been working on that past year. When someone is dissatisfied with his or her job, all sorts of attitudinal and behavioral consequences are likely to follow. (You could no doubt guess some of these, but it's nice to have empirical evidence to confirm our suspicions). Among those negative consequences are higher absenteeism, greater likelihood of turnover, and, of greater interest to us here, fewer "organizational citizenship" behaviors—things like being dependable, complying with company rules, advancing the company's goals, and being willing to respect and to help people.[1] The running realtor didn't seem like much of a "citizen" in my home, that's for sure. In fact, the way he was acting made me want to deport him!

For some people like this realtor, a golden calf is not the primary obstacle to Christlikeness in the workplace. A despised job is. Perhaps you can personally identify with what I'm talking about. Perhaps you live it every day. Or maybe you know somebody who fits that description. Tap into your own experience with this cause-and-effect relationship for a moment. How hard is it to be the model Christian when you can't stand what you're doing? For that matter, how hard is it to display *any* evidence that you've even *heard* about Jesus Christ? Nearly impossible. And it's almost as hard to reverse course here, since we hesitate to ask God for help. He's the last person we want to talk to after our misdemeanors because of the guilt we feel. We're supposed to act one way, and we're acting completely the opposite—all because of this job we can't stand. Who wants to face the Father while flailing in failure? Not me, that's for sure.

But I should. And so should you, because God has some options for us here—options that have the power to fix the situation permanently. What is Jesus' answer to a believer who hates his job? We find it in the second beatitude.

## MONDAY MOURNING ON THE MOUNT

They lived in a land that was not their own. It had not been since Rome took over decades earlier. Before that, it was the Greeks, the Persians, the Babylonians. Seldom had they known peace or freedom.

As were the others, the Romans were ruthless in their own way, slowly sapping the life from these people. The Emperor Pompey had desecrated the temple, their holiest place, and later installed Herod the Great—an Arab!—to be their "high priest." Under Herod, these people saw the children of Bethlehem slaughtered. Under Herod's son, they saw their prophet John the Baptist beheaded. Beyond these indignities, there were the economic realities. Very few of these people earned or owned much, especially after the tax collectors were through with them.

Life was cruel for God's chosen in the first century. Their religion, their children, their money, their latest prophet—their very hope—were all being stolen away by their captors.

In the midst of this maelstrom came a word from a lanky Rabbi. This man probably couldn't bench-press His own weight, but in that instant, He proved capable of lifting something far greater. With just one line, He began to lift their burden, supplanting it with optimism. "Don't fret over your condition" was His response to their pain, "for a new day is on the horizon. God knows your suffering, your public and your private suffering, and He'll remove every last bit of it."

Actually, He put it more succinctly and much more memorably: *"Blessed are those who mourn, for they will be comforted."*

It was both a reminder of what they had heard from the prophet Isaiah and a promise to fulfill Isaiah's prophecy:

> The Spirit of the Sovereign Lord is on me, because the Lord has anointed me to preach good news to the poor.

He has sent me to bind up the brokenhearted, to proclaim freedom for the captives and release from dark-
ness for the prisoners, to proclaim the year of the Lord's
favor and the day of vengeance of our God, to comfort
all who mourn. (Isaiah 61:1–2)

Comfort is ahead. Remember that. Jesus' response
when you hate your life condition is to turn your attention to hope—an eschatological hope, in the language of theologians. It's a hope for the future, a hope
for eternity, *a call to amend your current thinking.*
"When things are tough," He teaches us, "don't think
so much about your life circumstances. Think about
your *afterlife* circumstances."

It's a striking, unconventional remedy. If you can't
change your circumstances, change your mind. Look
ahead—*way* ahead. Embrace hope rather than mis-
ery. In the words of Paul, "I consider that our present
sufferings are not worth comparing with the glory
that will be revealed in us" (Romans 8:18).

---

*When things are tough, don't think so
much about your life circumstances. Think
about your afterlife circumstances.*

---

Despite all of its truth, for many people that's a
challenging lesson to put into practice. God's kingdom is such a fuzzy concept to some that they may
find it hard to tap into the power of Christ's invitation
here. If we knew more about what those "afterlife cir-

cumstances" entailed, perhaps we'd be better able to apply Jesus' solution to our mourning. Perhaps we'd be empowered to let tomorrow's comfort ease today's discomfort.

Well, actually, we are. We do know some things about the magnificence of the afterlife because God has revealed them to us. Since that is beyond my expertise, though, allow me defer to a specialist on the subject.

Erwin Lutzer, in his books on the attributes of heaven, does perhaps the best job encapsulating in lay language the Bible's glimpses of God's kingdom. Among his many helpful insights, based solidly on the book of Revelation, he explains that in heaven there will be no more hunger, no more thirst, no more exhaustion from our work. All of our needs will be met. In God's kingdom, there will be no more strife between nations. People will live in harmony with one another. There will be no more abominations. All those things that frustrate us because they contravene God's will are forever gone when we return home. Perhaps most notably, there will be no more death. We'll never again have to say good-bye to a friend or a relative. We'll never again have to worry about accidents and tragedies stealing loved ones away from us. In God's kingdom there is no more sorrow, no more crying, no more pain—ever.[2]

This is the type of comfort that awaits those who presently mourn. It's an extraordinary hope, if we take the time to think about it in such concrete terms, if we meditate on the specifics of what awaits us upon our arrival in the kingdom.

In the second beatitude, Jesus invites us to make

the time—most especially during our periods of mourning. It is His perfect answer to alleviate the pressure of our quite imperfect jobs. Look forward. Remain hopeful. Be expectant and thankful for what's ahead once this millisecond we call "life" ticks away.

## ANOTHER VEHICLE TO TOW YOUR WOE

The Bible has more to say on the question of how to overcome this obstacle of a despised job. In addition to the "confident hope" mind-set that Jesus teaches, *consider reevaluating just how important your job is—from God's perspective.* There are dimensions to almost every job that really do honor God. And focusing on those aspects can instantly improve one's life at work. Let me again defer to some of the better contemporary thinking to make this point.

Doug Sherman and William Hendricks nicely articulate some of these God-honoring dimensions in their widely read book, *Your Work Matters to God.* How does it matter? Among the ways are these: (1) Through your work, you serve people, (2) through your work, you meet your family's needs, and (3) through your work, you earn money to give to others.[3]

Did you ever think about your work in those terms before? Take number one, for example. It's a biggie. Did you ever stop to mentally list all the ways your work actually serves other people? Consider that realtor racing through my house, oppressed by the tyranny of the urgent, just trying to get to his next appointment and through his day. Does his presence in my house serve others? You bet! That same realtor eventually brought two couples through the house in the weeks that followed. He served an essential need

I had to get prospective buyers to look at the house. I wanted to sell it quickly to get to my new job in Virginia, and his work was helping me in that process.

Similarly, as he showed the house, he was helping his clients find just the right spot to raise their children. This was important, contributory work, but he wasn't thinking along those lines. Had he done so, he probably would have reaped the intrinsic satisfaction that so often accompanies service to others. His job probably would have been a lot more palatable—and, maybe, so would he.

Now, if those connections seem like a little bit of a leap to you, I can relate. I felt the same way after I first read Sherman and Hendricks. So I put this service-attitude connection to the test over the past couple of years. Beyond using it personally when my own job has been lackluster, I've tried it out on others as well. When an opportunity presents itself—when I meet someone who appears to hate his job—I offer him this "service" perspective on his work and pay close attention to his response. I have to admit, the results have been impressive.

Typical was a recent trip to the video store. When I got to the counter, I was assisted by a girl in her early twenties who seemed particularly unmotivated. "How are you tonight?" I asked somewhat automatically.

"I'll be better at eleven," she responded, scanning the videos.

Ah. An opportunity. "Not your ideal Saturday night, huh?"

"Yeah, that's an understatement."

"Well," I said, donning my researcher's cap, "I'll tell you something. Some of us sure appreciate the fact that you're here. It really makes our night better to have these videos. I don't know if that helps you any, but it's true."

She smiled and paused from her robotic scanning. "Actually, that does help," she replied, making eye contact for the first time. "It really does. Thanks."

Not the most scientific experiments, I know. But almost without exception, when I've pointed out the service aspect of somebody's job, that person seems refreshed by the comment. It puts the minutia and the routine into a new light. It makes the job better for a moment.

And that's a moment that you can create for yourself each time your work is getting you down. The work you perform serves people, and a daily reminder of how it serves people can plain and simple make your job better too. If it can happen at a video store, it can happen anywhere.

---

*Consider reevaluating just how important your job is—from God's perspective.*

---

In the same way, remaining mindful of numbers two and three on Sherman and Hendricks's list can help us adjust our attitude toward work. In God's eyes, it's an important accomplishment to meet our family's needs. As Paul writes to Timothy, "If anyone does not provide for his relatives, and especially for his immediate family, he has denied the faith and is worse than an unbeliever" (1 Timothy 5:8). Moreover, you can honor God in your work by taking some of that income and sharing it with others. Your work generates resources to meet financial needs that might otherwise go unmet. That matters.

Do you feel any of the tension draining yet? Maybe not, but let me ask it this way: Could any of these attitudinal techniques assist you tomorrow to hate your job a little less—and to model Christ a little more? You won't really know unless you try.

## WHAT ABOUT JUST QUITTING?

As a last resort, remember that there is nothing in Scripture that forbids you from taking another job. That may seem like a cop-out or a thoroughly secularized perspective on the situation, but it's really not. In fact, God may actually be using that dissatisfaction of yours to shepherd you into a position where you can better use the gifts He has given you. If you have concluded this through your conversations with Him, consider taking inventory of your gifts before you jump from one ship to another. Stop and evaluate what God has bestowed on you and what jobs might best fit that gift profile.

To assist you in this endeavor, we at Regent University have developed and validated a free-of-charge, on-line "spiritual gifts test," based on Paul's gift list in Romans 12. The website address is www.gifttest.org. It might be worth fifteen minutes of your time to professionally assess your attributes, so that if God is calling you to some other work, you may better discern what it is.

## THE SECRET TO A BETTER JOB
## AND A BETTER WITNESS

Hating your job can neutralize Christlikeness as much as can pride, greed, ambition, or any other golden calf. So if this obstacle resonates with you, make some time in your schedule to really consider the New Testament advice for the mourner. There's a lot at stake because Christians who remain in a despondent state are seldom effective witnesses.

In fact, they're usually just the opposite. Believe me, I didn't see Christ in the guy who was rude to me in my own home. I saw the antithesis of Christ. I saw somebody who didn't seem to care about anything but getting his job done. And, according to my realtor, he didn't much care about that either!

It didn't have to be that way for him, but he simply didn't know the secret. God has, in His grace, revealed fresh perspectives on work that can improve the quality of your work life—perspectives like keeping your trials in an eternal context and remaining mindful of how even the little things we do at work honor God by meeting others' needs. Road test those perspectives for yourself—even for just one week. They're biblical, so what do you have to lose? Be advised, though. If you do this in earnest, you'll probably notice a range of surprising and remarkable changes.

Some of those changes will be immediate—fewer restless nights, no more dreading the dusk of your weekend, an end to the daily countdown to quitting time, the rewarding feeling that your work actually has a purpose. Other changes—some of the larger ones—will accrue to you over time. In particular, your working conditions will no longer prevent you from modeling your faith on the job. You'll probably see positive effects on your productivity and on the quality of your work as well. And, importantly, you'll never again treat anyone like a china cabinet.

The secret that running realtor didn't know is this: God has made a pathway for our exodus from Monday "mourning." All we have to do is to run through it.

## Self-Check

When things seem hopeless, Jesus offers hope. In the midst of life's trials, have you ever tapped into that hope described in the second beatitude? Could setting your present difficulties against the backdrop of eternal comfort improve your situation?

What aspects of your work serve people? How does your work meet important needs and improve the quality of other people's lives? Might it make your job better if you thought of it as a service ministry rather than as just your job?

## NOTES

1. For some of the better studies along these lines, please see C. J. Cranny, Patricia Cain Smith, and Eugene F. Stone, *Job Satisfaction* (Lexington, Mass.: Lexington, 1992); Mel Schnake, "Organizational Citizenship: A Review, Proposed Model and Research Agenda," *Human Relations* 44 (1991): 735–59; Cheri Ostroff, "The Relationship Between Satisfaction, Attitudes and Performance: An Organizational-Level Analysis," *Journal of Applied Psychology* 77, no. 6 (1992): 963–74.

2. See chapter 5 of Erwin W. Lutzer, *One Minute After You Die* (Chicago: Moody, 1997).

3. See Doug Sherman and William Hendricks, *Your Work Matters to God* (Colorado Springs: NavPress, 1987), 87.

# Obstacle 3

# THE "MEEKNESS IS WEAKNESS" MYTH

*Blessed are the meek, for they
will inherit the earth.*

MATTHEW 5:5

Chances are, your pastor didn't graduate from Yale Divinity School (YDS). Neither did I, but as part of my professional development, I did spend two years there studying Christian theology. At least, that's what I thought I was getting myself into when I applied.

Take a quick tour with me, and I'll show you what I mean. Even before you enter the hallowed halls, you'll catch an eyeful of culture in the parking lot. The bumper stickers flash like warning signals alerting us to what's ahead:

"God is too big to fit inside one religion."

"In goddess we trust."

"Keep your rosaries off my ovaries."

That's hardly an appetizer. Let's stop in the private prayer chapel on our way to the classrooms. Kneel at the altar and open its large-print Bible. Then flip through the pages and peruse the variety of Scriptures the students have *crossed out* or *modified* to make God more politically correct.

When you're finished worshiping the goddess of Sarah and Rebekah, we'll pass the faculty offices as we head toward the classrooms. No, you're not seeing things. That is indeed euthanasia and lesbian rights propaganda plastered to some of the office doors. Nice complement to the students' bumper stickers, I guess.

We can also check out their exceptional library while we're in this wing of the building. The volume of resources is quite unique—as is the artwork. You can't miss the large crucifix in the stairwell. Yes, there's a naked woman on that cross. The caption reveals that her name is Christa.

Lastly, let's take a seat at the back of a lecture hall. Don't be shy. Visitors are more than welcome. Then listen closely. If we're lucky, we'll be in the presence of one of the few world-class scholars remaining at YDS. Chances are better than even, though, that we'll be immersed instead in political ideology and biblical revisionism. Genesis was largely written by someone called the "J-writer," and "J" was most likely a woman. We don't know who actually wrote the Gospels or whether Jesus *really* claimed to be divine. We do think, however, that He may have had homosexual relations with Lazarus. Herod the Great and the Pharisees were admirable men. And, by the way, "the majority" of New Testament scholars no longer believe that superstitious Resurrection story!

Welcome to a Christian seminary—Ivy League style. It's liberal theology at its finest. What I found most intriguing about YDS, though, is that countless students and faculty actually consider the place *conservative!* Even oppressively so. A primary reason is that Yale still requires its seminarians to take a full six credits of Old Testament and six credits of New Testament before graduation. Granted, that may not sound like a lot for prospective clergy—especially since in most U.S. seminaries, twelve credits will barely get you to Jeremiah.

However, Yale's reference group includes places like Princeton Theological Seminary, Harvard Divinity School, and Union Theological Seminary (New York City). These schools require even *less* Scripture study and boast student and faculty cultures that make Yalees seem like Reaganites. Hence, from a YDS point of view, the school is delivering theological education from a relatively conservative perspective.

Does this strike you as bizarre too? By most standards, these are bright people. *Really* bright. We're talking 1400+ on their SATs. Still, they're completely blind to something that should be patently obvious. They think the school culture is right wing when it's clearly left. Why do they get it exactly wrong? Because they are evaluating against man's standards—in this case, other schools—not God's standards.

Now notice something, if you would. *This is the same problem that plagues many workplace Christians when it comes to meekness.* We, too, get it exactly wrong. For some reason, many of us equate meekness with weakness. We think it's a shortcoming, a liability, a sign that someone doesn't have what it takes to succeed in the corporate world. But is it? God seems to have a very different perspective on meekness. In fact, as we'll see shortly, He takes the opposite viewpoint. Like those students at Yale, we get this completely backwards, and we get it backwards because we measure the value of meekness with man's standard, not God's.

Let's look at that standard and then see how the workplace keeps us from adopting it.

## GOD'S STANDARD OF MEEKNESS

When Jesus told the crowd, "Blessed are the meek, for they will inherit the earth," what did He mean by *meek?* Tapping the original translation and some other Scriptures will be illuminating. The word translated here as *meek* is the Greek word *praus.* It's a word that's usually translated as *gentle* in the New Testament. Therefore, Jesus is not communicating that "blessed are the wimpy," as we might infer from our contemporary usage of the word *meek.* Rather, it's more accurate to interpret the verse as "blessed are those of us who are *gentle.*"

We can go further with this word study. And as we do, we'll see just how pervasive this teaching is.

The directive toward gentleness is hardly a one-time appeal in the New Testament. It's anything but an obscure, offhand suggestion. Instead, the Greek root here, *prautes* (gentleness or humility), shows up in some of the most classic New Testament verses:

- "But the fruit of the Spirit is love, joy, peace, patience, kindness, goodness, faithfulness, gentleness *[prautes]* and self-control" (Galatians 5:22–23).
- "Therefore, as God's chosen people, holy and dearly loved, clothe yourself with compassion, kindness, humility, gentleness *[prautes]* and patience" (Colossians 3:12).
- "Brothers, if someone is caught in a sin, you who

are spiritual should restore him gently *[prautes]*" (Galatians 6:1).

- "Always be prepared to give an answer to everyone who asks you to give the reason for the hope that you have. But do this with gentleness *[prautes]* and respect" (1 Peter 3:15).

Repeatedly we hear that gentleness should be our calling card. It's an indicator that the Spirit is at work in our lives. It's how we are to teach others and how we are to evangelize. It's nothing less than a distinguishing characteristic of the maturing Christian.

Hard to believe? Here's even clearer evidence that growing in Christlikeness entails gentleness. Jesus seldom used adjectives to describe Himself. When He did, though, look at the very first descriptor He chose: "Take my yoke upon you and learn from me, for I am gentle *[praus]* and humble in heart" (Matthew 11:29).

---

*First and foremost, Jesus*
*called Himself gentle.*

---

First and foremost, Jesus called Himself gentle. That's worth contemplating. To emulate Jesus Christ, consider His disposition. It was gentle. Consider His approach to sinners. It was gentle. Consider how He typically handled conflict and adversity. Gently. Consider how He invited—and continues to invite—people to know God through knowing Him. Gently. *He* is God's standard of meekness.

Following Jesus Christ, then, means consistently growing in gentleness. It is to become increasingly meek. That means for many of us, it is to change dispositions—in some cases, to *radically* change.

## GOD CAN HELP *ANYONE* BECOME MEEK

That may seem unrealistic, but such change in persona is possible—and here's one way we know. Look again at that list of gentleness verses above. Did you notice who authored the last one? I've always been struck by 1 Peter 3:15, not so much because it tells us to be prepared with an apologetic defense of the gospel as because it is *Peter* who is teaching on gentleness. Do you find that at all peculiar? Let's face it, from what we read about Peter in the Gospels, this is not the guy you want teaching in your nursery school. He's more akin to a principal in an out-of-control high school who walks the halls while wielding a bat and a bullhorn. He'd sooner cut off an ear than lend one. I'd also hazard to guess that the preferred method of evangelism for this crass fisherman would not be gentleness and respect. He'd probably be more comfortable slapping someone across the face with a trout and threatening eternal damnation.

But here he is in verse 15 discarding the bullhorn and the trout. We see a 180-degree reversal in his approach to human relations. That's significant, especially for those of us who have Peter's persona. If you think becoming meeker is impossible because you've never been that way, take note of a two-thousand-year-old miracle: Jesus softened someone like Peter, so He can soften you and me.

Transformation is but a prayer and a decision

away. Ask and choose to become a gentler person, and then persist in your effort to grow. Be advised, though, that the lion's den of the workplace has a way of stunting that growth. So if you genuinely desire this transformation to take root at work, you may have to overcome an obstacle other than your Peter-like personality—a powerful and persuasive obstacle.

## THE PRIMARY OBSTACLE TO MEEKNESS IN THE WORKPLACE

If God says that meekness is a virtue and He wants us to change, why, then, are there so few meek Christians in the workplace? What is it about the work environment that inhibits us from adopting a gentle, Christlike disposition? John, one of my fifty-year-old graduate students, offered me this insight.

"Once upon a time in my career," he told me, "I really did try to let my values affect my decision making and the way I dealt with people. I'd even silently ask myself questions like 'What does God want me to do here?' and 'What decision would Jesus make here?' Now, twenty-five years later, the questions I ask at work are different—more like 'What's company policy here?' 'What will get me the biggest bonus?' and 'How can we get the work done faster?' The other day I even chewed out a guy—*a single dad*—for showing up five minutes late! When I thought about that at my desk later, I realized just how much I've changed. Some days I don't even know who I am anymore."

How did this happen? At the beginning of his career, John was essentially a God-centered employee. Then, one morning decades later, he woke up and didn't recognize the person staring back at him in the mirror. Nor did he like him very much.

What John experienced is not at all uncommon. Some jobs and some work environments do change us. They have an invisible mechanism called the corporate culture that tends to shape us in its own secular image. Perhaps you've felt the grate of its sandpaper slowly eroding your own Christian values.

Workplace researchers have studied this transformational process since the 1920s, and their conclusions are helpful. In a nutshell (yes, I'm going to attempt to summarize eighty years of research in a paragraph or two), they've found that when we start a job with a new company, we become socialized into that environment. Basically, through formal orientations and training programs, and through informal interaction with our new co-workers, we feel pressure to modify our attitudes, expectations, and behaviors to better fit in. In essence, we adjust a little of who we are. Over time, we, like John, may end up adjusting *a lot* of who we are.

Note that this is far from deliberate or even conscious. Even if we have no desire to let a job shape us, extended marination in the corporate culture can still do so. John did not intentionally morph into a person he disliked. He had no strategic plan to become a more aggressive, insensitive, and demanding individual. After years of working in that environment, though, he became a product of it. He became like many of the people around him, conforming to their values and their priorities.

That is exactly what the best research predicts will happen when we work closely with others for a prolonged period of time.[1] Interestingly, it's also what the apostle Paul predicted.

## PAUL'S INSIGHTS ON CORPORATE CULTURE

Paul apparently had a nineteen-hundred-year jump on my ivory tower colleagues. He appropriated for the Corinthian church a line from a then-popular Greek play and inserted it into the canon. Because of its timeless applicability, we should also insert this principle into our mental database: "Bad company corrupts good character" (1 Corinthians 15:33). Be careful about who you hang out with, Paul says. You just might start thinking and acting like they do. Another workplace researcher, "Dr. Solomon" of Jerusalem University, imparted similar wisdom centuries earlier: "He who walks with the wise grows wise, but a companion of fools suffers harm" (Proverbs 13:20).

So how does all this apply to the virtue of meekness? Think about your work environment. Are you a companion of meek people? Think about what it takes for you to climb the corporate ladder. Is it gentleness and humility? Think about what's required for you to get a hefty merit raise. Are the meek—or the aggressive—rewarded more handsomely where you work?

---

*The work environment can subtly shape us to be the polar opposite of meek.*

---

Most of us know this intuitively, but we need an occasional reminder. The work environment—its socialization process, its reward system, its demands for faster, better performance—can subtly shape us to be the polar opposite of meek. Even worse, after years of this indoctrination, many of us actually become convinced that meekness is a *negative* trait. *Meekness is weakness,* we rationalize. *That's just the way it is in business today.* So we continue along this road, measuring ourselves against man's standard of meekness, not God's.

And then one morning we wake up strangers to ourselves, having bought into a dangerous, culture-driven myth.

If that describes you, if you have unconsciously adopted the counterscriptural perspective that equates meekness with weakness, then it's probably time to dispel that myth once and for all. If you think you can't be meek on the job because meek employees get stepped on, get passed over for promotions, or miss out on valuable rewards, think again. Think like God thinks.

Jesus set the record straight about the meek. They will "inherit the earth."

He said that the Supreme Evaluator smiles on the gentle and rewards them well. "Don't worry about that promotion," He says. "I have a *real* promotion in store for you. Stay on course! Persevere! Don't be corrupted by whatever 'bad company' may be near you. Follow in My gentle footsteps and your reward—your inheritance—will far exceed that title and 6 percent raise you missed."

Look in your own mirror. Has the work world convinced you that meekness is weakness? God replies that meekness is maturity.

Has the work world convinced you that meekness is foolishness? God replies through Paul, "The foolishness of God is wiser than men" (1 Corinthians 1:25 NASB).

Has the work world convinced you that meekness undermines career success? God replies by raising up a counterexample in the most unlikely of places: the football gridiron.

## A TESTIMONY TO THE STRENGTH OF MEEKNESS

Like those students at Yale Divinity School, this man thought he was something that he was not. He, too, was measuring by man's standard, not God's.

Because he regularly attended a church, Tom Landry thought he was a Christian. In his own words: "I had been in and about church my whole life. But really, it was only half-heartedly. . . . I thought of myself as a Christian but I really wasn't. I was just a churchgoer, which is a lot different. If you just go to church, it's a lot like going to the Lion's Club or something like that. Oh, man, there's no comparison."[2] Then one day in 1959, Landry accepted an invitation to a men's Bible study because, he says, he couldn't think of a graceful way to get out of it![3] It's a good thing too, since in that meeting Tom came to realize how many passages from the Sermon on the Mount spoke directly to the personal struggles in his life. So he returned the next week. And the next. Later that year, Tom says, "I finally reached a point where faith outweighed the doubts, and I was willing to commit my entire life to God."[4]

In 1959, Tom was a thirty-three-year-old assistant coach for the New York Giants and an off-season insurance salesman. Eventually, he would coach a team of his own—the Dallas Cowboys—and would lead them to an unprecedented twenty consecutive winning seasons, five Super Bowl appearances, and two championships. An impressive record, to say the least. Even more impressive to many of us who watched him, though, was that he did it without raising his voice.

Tom was meek in the best sense of the word. He was a reserved man, a soft-spoken man, a man who walked with God as he walked the sidelines. That was evident by his game-time manner. Were the Cowboys up by 14 or down by 14? Tom's demeanor provided no clue. Was it fourth and goal on the opponent's one-yard line or first and ten on their own twenty? Did the Cowboys just fumble away the game? Did the refs just blow a call? Don't look to Tom's expression for answers. This now-devout Christian personified gentleness and self-control.

Not exactly the norm in the workplace of NFL coaching. More typical were people like legendary Vince Lombardi, infamous for being unapproachable *for days* after his offense had a bad game.[5] Similarly, Raider coach John Madden got so worked up in his job that he had to retire from coaching because of ulcers.[6] Chicago Bears coach Mike Ditka also fit the mold. Not only was he notorious for his sideline tantrums, but Ditka was apparently a bear off the field as well. When he played tennis with Landry, for example, he would smash his racket on the ground so many times it began to resemble, in Tom's words, an "aluminum pretzel."[7]

But Tom was different. According to sportswriter

Bob St. John: "The pressures of coaching in the NFL have had adverse mental and physical effects on the majority of coaches in the profession. But Landry does not . . . have ulcers or trouble sleeping."[8] Tom attributes that to his faith, asserting that "my relationship with Christ gives me a source of power I would not have otherwise. What eats you up inside is fear and anxiety. God does not give us fear, but power and love and self-control."[9]

That's meekness.

Tom Landry managed to remain meek in a world of macho football players, thunderous peers, and a hypercritical football town. The culture of his workplace put no edge on the man. Tom did not allow it to shape him adversely. Rather, he was shaped daily by his faith. As a result, today Tom Landry is renowned not only for his win-loss record, but for being a contemporary role model for workplace Christians everywhere. His legacy is one of both character and success.

Ours can be too if we reject the notion that meekness is weakness. Don't buy into the workplace myth. In gentleness, you can both survive and thrive in a job environment that continually encourages you to act otherwise. As discussed in chapter 1, this begins by acknowledging God as your ultimate CEO. It continues by taking a page from Coach Landry's playbook: Never lose sight of Jesus' disposition. Regardless of what others are doing on the job, don't let harshness, quick-temperedness, and aggressiveness undermine your witness and your legacy. Instead, live by God's standard: "I am gentle and humble in heart."

No, meekness is not weakness. It's Christlikeness.

## Self-Check

Think about your previous workweek. In what situations and with which people did you fall short of God's standard of meekness? What might have been different at work last week had you been as meek as Jesus encouraged us to be? How would your gentler behavior have impacted others and yourself?

Almost every work environment has elements that encourage us to be aggressive rather than meek. Can you identify the aspects of your job that push you in the wrong direction? And could you think of ways to resist those temptations and instead respond to God's call to be more gentle?

## NOTES

1. See, for example, J. R. Barker, "Tightening the Iron Cage: Concertive Control in Self-managed Teams," *Administrative Science Quarterly* 38 (1993): 408–37.

2. Bob St. John, *The Landry Legend: Grace Under Pressure* (Dallas: Word, 1989), 154.

3. Tom Landry and Gregg Lewis, *Tom Landry: An Autobiography* (New York: Walter, 1990), 109.

4. Ibid., 112.

5. Ibid., 102.

6. St. John, *The Landry Legend*, 159.

7. Landry and Lewis, *Tom Landry*, 266.

8. St. John, *The Landry Legend*, 159.

9. Ibid.

## Obstacle 4

# A "FIGHT FOR YOUR RIGHTS" MENTALITY

*God blesses those who are hungry
and thirsty for justice, for they
will receive it in full.*

MATTHEW 5:6 NLT

If ever there were someone who hungered and thirsted for man-made justice, it was Donald Drusky.

Drusky was an employee of U.S. Steel in the 1960s and a member of the United Steelworkers of America, Local 1219. After a dispute with his employer and union over $2,500 he claimed was owed to him, Drusky publicly protested, picketing outside the company gates. This performance neither amused nor intimidated U.S. Steel, which promptly sent Drusky on a permanent vacation. They probably suspected that Drusky's next move could be a lawsuit, but they could have hardly estimated Drusky's appetite for justice.

Drusky first went to the National Labor Relations Board (NLRB), the federal agency that oversees the relationship among companies, unions, and union members. He filed a complaint alleging unfair labor practices by both his employer and his union. Then he filed another. And then another. Three years later,

Drusky had filed an unprecedented *375 complaints* in all. Equally unprecedented was that the NLRB dismissed *every one* of his claims as unmeritorious: 0-for-375.[1] You'd think he'd get the message.

He didn't. As his string of goose eggs mounted, Drusky tried a different tactic, suing the regional director of the NLRB—the person responsible for dismissing his complaints. A federal court wasted little time dispensing with these allegations as well: 0-for-376.[2]

This was "equal justice under law"? Drusky didn't buy it. His rights had been violated, and somebody had to pay. So he set his sights on those charged with guaranteeing him that equal justice. Drusky sued the *entire federal judiciary*, claiming that they had conspired to deprive him of his rights. Calling that case "frivolous," the court again left Drusky famished and parched: 0-for-377.[3]

Well, maybe suing a different set of lawyers would bear edible fruit. Drusky next sued the American Bar Association for its part in the conspiracy. But again, an adverse court decision yielded not a crumb of satisfaction for Drusky: 0-for-378.[4]

Had Donald Drusky tasted enough defeat? Perhaps he had for a while. But in 1998, a full thirty years after his quest began, Drusky filed a lawsuit that produced a cornucopia of headlines worldwide.

Drusky sued God.

I kid you not. Starving for retribution and tired of waiting for God to intervene on his behalf, Drusky filed suit in the U.S. District Court, blaming God for refusing to remedy what U.S. Steel had done to him decades earlier. In that same action, Drusky also threw the rest of the spaghetti at the wall to see what might stick. He sued former Presidents Reagan and Bush, the television networks, all fifty states, the Federal Communications Commission, all federal judges (again), the 100th through 105th Congresses, and you and me. That's right. In this action Drusky sued every person in America for sitting idly by during his ordeal. (Apparently, then, God is not only our Co-pilot, He's also our Co-defendant!)

The main target of the suit, though, was Drusky's Creator. The allegation read in part: "Defendant God is the sovereign ruler of the universe and took no corrective action against the leaders of his Church and his Nation for their extremely serious wrongs, which ruined the life of Donald S. Drusky."[5]

What recompense did Drusky want for God's failure to cater? I guess he could have asked for the moon. Instead, Drusky merely asked God to return his youth, to resurrect his mother and pet pigeon (complete with halo), and to grant Drusky "the guitar playing skills of the famous guitarists." On the more socially conscious side, Drusky also insisted that God let someone find a cure for cancer and that He return Abraham Lincoln "to serve as Your ambassador from Heaven to make a better America and world."

Will God restore Drusky's job? Or will He respond as He did to Job? Stay tuned, friends. The decision follows these brief announcements from the Defendant's best-selling Book.

## BEWARE OF A "FIGHT FOR YOUR RIGHTS" MENTALITY

Conflict. It's inevitable in our lives. Somewhere, somehow, someday soon, if not today, something will

strike you as unjust. Unfair. Unconscionable. It's un-
avoidable.

God cares about how we react to conflict, and He
wants us to react in a manner that honors Him. But
first things first. How we *react* to conflict is often de-
termined by how we *think* about conflict. So, given
that precursor, I ask you: When something unfair
happens to you, what dominates your thoughts? Is it
the question: "What is a God-honoring approach to
this problem?"

When an inconsiderate driver cuts you off, do you
think about honoring God? When a neighbor's fence
encroaches on your yard or his dog chews up your
garden, do your thoughts turn to God's will? If you
were fired for a wrongful reason, would honoring God
be at its rightful place in your mind?

More than likely, the first thing that would come
to mind in such situations (and often the middle
thing and the last thing!) would be a different kind of
question—something like, "What rights do I have
here?" You have the right to some space on the road.
You have the right to keep your property fence- and
canine-free. You have the right to retain your job (or
so you might think) unless there's just cause to fire
you. And when those kind of rights have been violated, by default there's the tendency to begin thinking
about how to get what's "fair"—what's owed to you by
others. This is how people typically think about such
conflicts and, like I said, how we *think* about conflict
usually determines how we *react* to it.

*When we focus on getting what we're
owed, we abandon our focus on
resolving conflicts God's way.*

This is a problem for any Christian who desires to model Jesus Christ. When we have a hunger and thirst to secure our rights—to be treated fairly and equitably—then we are in jeopardy of compromising two vital things that God cares about. First, *we tend to compromise our witness as Christians.* When we adopt a fight-for-your-rights mentality, worldly rules guide us. Worldly motives abide in us. We'll get even with those who chide us, now that Satan has made progress inside us.

Poetics aside us (sorry), there is a genuine danger in permitting rights, equity, and fairness to become our gods—our "personal golden calf" in the vernacular of chapter 1. When we focus on getting what we're owed (whether at work, at home, or anywhere else), we abandon our focus on resolving conflicts God's way. Instead, a man-made approach to dealing with problematic people becomes our approach. Society's rules of engagement become our rules. And then the upshot: When the lord of rights replaces the Lord of Might, our conflicts often culminate in broken relationships and marred witness.

And that's just when we *win.* If we don't get what's coming to us, *we may compromise not only our relationships with others, but also our relationship with*

*God.* Do you think Donald Drusky was audacious in suing God? For demanding that God intervene on his behalf? I do too, but in point of fact, Drusky's resentment of God is not that far removed from some of our own. We may never formalize the grievance in district court. We may never insist on a haloed pigeon (although the bird would be a neat conversation piece). But when we hunger and thirst for the world to be fair—*and when despite our best efforts it still turns out to be unfair*—we may develop a hidden, unspoken grudge against God for it. After all, as Drusky said, God is sovereign. God is all-powerful. God could have done something about this problem, right? Why hasn't He?

Notice the drift from reverence to resentment? It all begins with a rights-oriented mind-set. It all begins by focusing on what we think we're owed by others and by God. Almost everyone in our contemporary culture is at risk. Are you?

## TAKE A BRIEF SELF-EXAM

That question might be a little tough to answer in the abstract, so let me make it a little plainer by putting it in a workplace context. Take this self-graded quiz, if you would. Don't think too long about these statements. Just mentally react to them and take note of your reaction. There are no trick questions here— just self-diagnosis—so be honest with yourself.

Here's the first one: A co-worker has stolen a great idea of yours and claimed it as his own. And now he's been rewarded for it. What's your initial reaction? Pause for a moment and think about it. Is your reaction closer to "Fight for my rights" or "How do I handle this in a God-honoring manner?"

Try this one: You received a lower percentage raise than someone else who is doing similar-quality work. He got 4 percent; you got 2. You worked just as many hours and were just as productive. What goes through your mind first? Are you thinking about what's owed to you and how you can secure it? Or are your thoughts more in the realm of emulating Christ through your reaction?

How about these? A co-worker regularly receives preferential treatment when the boss makes up the schedule. You were passed over for a promotion when you had clearly earned it. You were taunted by co-workers because of your faith. You patiently served one of those impossible customers only to learn that the customer later complained about *your* attitude to the supervisor—and the incident gets written up in your file. What's your reaction?

End of quiz. Beginning of confession: If you're like me (and like most people who have been indoctrinated by the American culture), your reflex in these situations is to think in terms of your rights—in terms of what's equitable and what you can do to get what's coming to you. How can you level the playing field again?

Jerry stole your great idea? Expose him and claim what was yours to begin with.

A raise that's less than that of your co-workers? Demand fairness from the boss (or find a covert way of making up that 2 percent—you know, "borrow" some company supplies, make some personal long-distance phone calls on the company's bill, that sort of thing).

Unfair schedule? Complain until everyone else has to work as many Saturdays as you do.

Passed over for a promotion? Threaten to sue and then dust off your résumé.

Ridiculed because of your faith? Add that to the lawsuit, as well, or just even the score by ridiculing them right back.

One part obnoxious customer, one part obnoxious supervisor? Two parts reduced effort.

It's only fair.

That's just the problem, though. Especially on the job, our thoughts and behavior tend to be governed by what we think is fair, by what rights we think we have. And as a result, the guiding principle when we're faced with injustice is to *recover what's due*. In the world's eyes, that's perfectly legitimate—even encouraged—since today, so-called victims are martyred heroes! But as we heroes adopt a "fight for your rights" mentality, we start to look less and less like the persons who were singing in the pews a mere twenty-four hours earlier. Not very heroic.

It doesn't have to be that way. There's another approach to thinking about conflict, as Jesus showed us in the fourth beatitude—an approach that demonstrates to everyone around us what it *really* means to sit in one of those pews.

## FACING GOD IN THE FACE OF CONFLICT

Although most modern versions of Scripture render Matthew 5:6 as "Blessed are those who hunger and thirst for righteousness," one of the more recent translations exchanges the term *justice* for *righteousness*. That's not a stylistic exchange. The wording shift is intended to reflect the plainer meaning of the beatitude when heard in proper context—the literary and cultural context.

The scene was a crowd of Israelites who were depressed and demoralized. They were a people longing for God to act. So Jesus lifted some words from Psalm 107 to lift them up. Specifically, He borrowed from the following:

> They [in the desert on the way to Canaan] were hungry and thirsty, and their lives ebbed away. Then they cried out to the LORD in their trouble, and he delivered them from their distress. . . . for he satisfies the thirsty and fills the hungry with good things. (Psalm 107:5–6, 9)

These are verses offering hope to the oppressed, satisfaction to the subjugated. *God will respond,* these verses say. It seems that Jesus paraphrased this particular passage because it spoke directly to the condition of those hearing His sermon—people who were enduring daily injustice under Roman occupation.

In context, then, the fourth beatitude appears to be more about justice than about personal righteousness.[6] Hence, the translational shift. Its message is that God will deliver us from all of our suffering. Be patient, wait for God to work, and remain confident throughout that His brand of justice will ultimately prevail. "Stay hopeful amid your conflicts," Jesus was telling the crowd. "Don't sin in response to those conflicts. God knows how unfairly life is treating you, and in His time, He will fill your hunger with 'good things.'"

Right . . . (commence eye rolling and head shaking). Tell that to the guy who just lost his job and can't pay the mortgage. Tell that to the woman being sexually harassed every day by her boss. Tell that to the battered wife and her children. Tell that to just about anyone who has been wronged and has immediate needs that are going unmet. They might reply: "Hope doesn't put food on the table or protect us from pond-scum predators, buddy. Is this beatitude really about taking it on the chin and doing nothing while waiting for God to act? Sounds kind of escapist to me. Sounds like it just opens the door for evil to prevail all the more."

Fair point, if that's what you're thinking. It's easy to misinterpret the instruction of this beatitude, so let me be clear about this. I have found nothing in Scripture that *requires* us to automatically abdicate our man-made rights. There's nothing that commands us to disregard personal abuse or danger. That's not Jesus' intent here. Rather, as with the previous Beatitudes, Jesus is teaching in verse 6 about an *attitude* we should adopt. A mind-set. A principle that is to guide our thinking when times are tough.

The principle is this: When conflict and injustice come into your life, remember that God ultimately rights all wrongs. *If you think this way, you'll be less likely to sin in response to the injustice.* Life's unfairness won't undercut your effort to conduct yourself as Jesus would. Mistreatment won't tarnish your witness. You won't be like so many other people in the world who are more rights centered than God centered. Instead, if you take Jesus' invitation to heart, when something unfair happens to you, you'll think about how to han-

dle the situation in a God-honoring manner before
you consider any man-made rights you have.

---

*In the midst of conflict, you can be rights
centered or you can be God centered.
Each is an obstacle to the other.*

---

If that approach to conflict sounds a bit radical to
you, you're in good company. The same message
probably sounded radical to the Corinthian Christians when Paul told them to relinquish their right to
sue one another. Not wanting unbelievers to see dis-
sension among Christians, Paul says to his litigious
friends, "Why not rather be wronged? Why not rather
be cheated?" (1 Corinthians 6:7). Fire your lawyers.
Put down your weapons. Effective witness is more
important than your rights.

The same message probably sounded radical to
the Romans too, when Paul restated this teaching:
"Do not be overcome by evil, but overcome evil with
good" (Romans 12:21). When conflict comes your
way, focus more on modeling Christ and less on how
you've been wronged. Only then can you possibly
hope to repay evil with good.

And the same message probably sounded radical
to Jesus' captivated audience, especially when He
built on this beatitude by giving them specific appli-
cations of it.

"If someone strikes you on the right cheek, turn to
him the other also" (Matthew 5:39).

*But I have the right to strike him back,* they probably thought.

"And if someone wants to sue you and take your
tunic, let him have your cloak as well" (Matthew
5:40).

*But I have the right to defend myself,* they probably
thought.

"If someone forces you to go one mile" (the dis-
tance Roman soldiers could force Israelites to carry
their gear), "go with him two miles" (Matthew 5:41).

*But under Roman law, I have the right to stop after
one mile!*

The point is this: The New Testament presents a
clear and consistent message regarding how to think
about the conflicts that come your way. When life
treats you unfairly, you have a choice. You can be
rights centered or you can be God centered. Each is
an obstacle to the other.

### WITNESSING WITHOUT THE WITNESS BOX

And now back to our show.

A mere three weeks after Drusky filed his suit
against God, the judge had made his decision.

Three weeks? That's remarkable in today's justice
system! How so soon? Did Drusky finally have his
slam dunk? Maybe God didn't show up in court, so
the judge sided with Drusky on that technicality.

Not quite. The rapid disposition of this case simply reflected its lack of merit. Judge Norman Mordue
threw out Drusky's novel gravel as "nonsensical" and
"frivolous." Drusky's hunger and thirst for justice
would remain unsatisfied once again.

But that doesn't have to be the case for us. Our

Supreme Judge never throws out our case. He never dismisses our plea as "nonsensical" or "frivolous." We believers always have the privilege of pleading our case to the Highest Authority in the land, in complete confidence that justice *will* be done. Perhaps not on our timetable and perhaps not in the manner we would script, but justice will be done. For those of us hungering and thirsting for God's justice, we "will receive it in full." That's the mind-set that paves the way to handling conflict in a God-honoring manner.

Let me wrap this up by illustrating this mind-set in action. At two different universities, I have been involved in situations where, because of building renovations, my faculty colleagues and I have had to select new offices. In both cases, some faculty would get window offices, but others would not. In the first case, a faculty member of average seniority—and less-than-average Christian commitment—made clear from the outset that she *would* get a window office. To quote verbatim her humble request: "If I don't get a window, I'll scream!" She got her window office. In fact, she got an office with two windows.

In the second case, the most senior person in the department—a devout Christian—was appointed to assign offices to us. After he solicited our preferences, it became apparent that no one wanted the office that had no windows. So he took it. He had every right to the best office in the suite. He selected the worst.

A rights-centered mentality. A God-centered mentality. One inhibits Christlikeness, the other exhibits Christlikeness. One is "fair," the other is rare.

Focusing on fairness is a frequent flaw of the faithful. It's a correctable one, though. So the next time you experience some type of mistreatment, whether large or small, stop and reflect for a moment. *Think about what you're thinking about.* Mind what's coming to mind. Then, if you find yourself adopting a rights-centered mentality, try an experiment. Pray that through this conflict God will guide your thoughts, your words, and your actions. Even your facial expressions. Pray it often. And as you do, think about what's really at stake. Unbelievers will evaluate your claims for Christ most closely when you are under pressure, not when things are going well. If you react to conflict like most others do—through arguing, complaining, gossiping, litigating, and silent treatments—then unbelievers are unlikely to see God through you. Instead, they'll probably consider you a hypocrite and see little value in Christianity.

If, on the other hand, you don't permit the pursuit of fairness to be an obstacle to Christlikeness, you'll present the most powerful of testimonies. Like my colleague at the second university, you will model what others might never read for themselves in the Gospels. You may also preserve and nurture some essential relationships in the process—not the least of which is your relationship with God.

The workplace can be a hotbed of conflict and individual rights. And although God doesn't always require that we stand idly by when we've been wronged, *He does always want us to handle conflicts in a way that reflects His nature.* Avoiding a "fight for your rights" mentality makes that possible.

## Self-Check

Here's a pretty easy question: What's unfair in your life—whether at work, at home or anywhere else?

Here are some harder questions: What is that unfairness doing to you as an employee, as a parent, as a spouse . . . as a Christian? How is it affecting your relationship with others and with God?

Here's the hardest question: Will you consider the scriptural advice to let go of your right to be angry and to simply turn over the injustice to God?

When you stop keeping score and stop trying to secure what you're owed, God has a way of making all things work out for the good of those who love Him.

### NOTES

1. *Drusky v American Bar Association,* 77 LRRM 2407 (Northern District of Illinois 1971)

2. *Drusky v Henry Shore, Regional Director, Sixth Region, NLRB,* 67 LRRM 2990 (Western District of Pennsylvania 1968)

3. *Drusky v Judges of the Supreme Court,* 324 F.Supp. 332 (Western District of Pennsylvania 1971)

4. *Drusky v American Bar Association,* 74 LRRM 2543 (Western District of Pennsylvania 1970)

5. John O'Brien, "U.S. Court Casts Out Suit Against God," *Herald American* (Syracuse, New York) 14 March 1999, sec. B, p. 1.

6. For further illumination of this point, please consult Donald A. Hagner, *Matthew 1–13,* vol. 33A of *Word Biblical Commentary,* ed. David A. Hubbard, Glen W. Barker, John D. W. Watts (Old Testament), and Ralph P. Martin (New Testament) (Dallas: Word, 1993), 93.

# Obstacle 5

# COMPASSION FATIGUE

*Blessed are the merciful,*
*for they will be shown mercy.*
MATTHEW 5:7

At 6:30 one spring morning, my four-year-old son Michael proudly marched out to the front lawn to retrieve the morning paper. It was his new job, and he did it flawlessly. Walk to the end of the path, pick up the paper, bring it back. No problem, right? Well, this particular morning he decided to insert another step. Through the window I watched him pick up the paper and then look to the sky. He stared upward and remained motionless for about sixty seconds.

Seldom had anything other than Barney the Dinosaur held his attention that long, so I went out to see it for myself. There in the sky, slightly south of our home, were three news helicopters, hovering over the railroad tracks. They were documenting a tragedy—a tragedy that happened only five hundred yards from my house but made headlines around the world.

Four hours earlier that morning, a terrified conductor of an Amtrak train hit the horn and pulled the emergency brake. I didn't hear it, but the thirty-second screech woke Anne Graney, whose property was closer to the tracks than was mine. Graney would later tell the local newspaper, "At night, you don't hear train whistles unless there's something on the track."[1] Something was—or more correctly—someone. Julia Toledo was a forty-seven-year-old Ecuadorian immigrant and mother of four sons. All of them stood in the pathway of the train. All of them were struck at seventy-one miles per hour. The train engineer would later say that as he approached, three of the boys and their mother were on the south side of the tracks and the smallest son was on the north. Julia ran to save her baby, and all of her other sons followed in a panic.

Firefighters reported that the accident scene was horrific. Julia and three of the boys, ages three, six, and eleven, were killed instantly. The ten-year-old brother, Jose, arrived at Bridgeport Hospital in a coma, only to succumb two days later. Lying amid the shattered bodies were school backpacks, a small tennis shoe, and a Sesame Street figurine.

The tragedy shook our Connecticut community to its core. It made no sense at all. What in the world was this family doing on the tracks at that hour? Where could they possibly have been going? To this day people can only speculate. Some things about Julia we did learn, however.

Julia spent a lot of time at Caroline House, an education center for immigrant women run by Catholic nuns. Her youngest son, Pedro, would play in the daycare area while his mother learned English. But Julia was much more than just a student. Sister Brenda Lynch recalled for the media the recent Caroline

House Christmas party where Julia promised to bring a turkey, even though she had no money to do so. When she missed two classes in a row before the party, many assumed that Julia wouldn't be coming. The party began without her. Then a woman, peering through a window, spotted Julia on the street, walking toward Caroline House with a large turkey balanced on a platter. She wore a triumphant smile, and her sons marched in step behind her.

This was typical of Julia. When Valentine's Day rolled around, the nuns were perplexed when Julia inquired about how to order flowers. Still, they gave her the information. To their surprise, the nuns later received a bouquet of carnations with a note expressing Julia's love and gratitude.[2]

To support her family, Julia worked as a custodian at Fairfield University—my employer at the time. She covered the 4:00 P.M. to midnight shift, necessitating a lot of baby-sitting. Sister Maureen Fleming recalled that the baby-sitting became a hopeless problem. In fact, for a full week before the accident, Julia simply did not show up for work because she had no one to care for her children.

Compounding this, Julia's ex-husband was allegedly menacing her and threatening to take the children back to Ecuador. That might have been why she fled. She also was having problems with her landlord and was forced into a transitional YMCA housing shelter. But why the train tracks? The best explanation I heard was from Sister Bernadette, who told me that in the mountain towns of Ecuador where Julia had lived almost her entire life it's common for travelers to walk along train tracks since the tracks are typically the flattest and most direct route.

I also talked with Julia's co-workers. They were my co-workers too. Those who knew her well were as stunned by the tragedy as I was. Some knew Julia was having difficulties, but none seemed to grasp the magnitude of those problems until it was too late.

I sat with all of these people at the funeral. It was a very foreign venue for me—a Mormon church, a Spanish service, janitors and nuns flanking me. I couldn't understand a word that was said from the pulpit, but the facial expressions, the uncontrollable sobs, the prolonged hugs required no translator.

At the front of the room were three caskets. It was a poignant reminder of the family's poverty. They couldn't afford individual caskets, so Julia was buried with her three-year-old, the two middle sons lay together, and the oldest lay alone. On the exterior of the caskets were personal messages written in indelible marker at the wake. That, too, seemed fitting. Friends, family, classmates, and even strangers wrote of the indelible impression the victims had made on their own lives. They wrote about love. They wrote about laughter. They wrote about God. They said their good-byes.

Perhaps most moving were the large photos of five bright, smiling faces near the caskets. Midway through the service, a young boy cried, and his father carried him out. Everyone seemed to be thinking the same thing: A week ago the Toledo boys were just as boisterous. Dozens of heads turned toward those photos.

I left that place shaken, thinking about the power each one of us has to affect the lives of our co-workers. I was also struck by a cold reality about Julia's workplace. Julia—a person in dire need—worked around *thousands* of people who identify themselves as Christian. She worked in a Christian school whose mission is "to foster ethical and religious values and a sense of social responsibility." She worked every day around well-paid Christian employees and well-to-do Christian students. But no one there had any more than a superficial relationship with her. No one seemed to know of her need. All it would have taken was for *one* of these Christians to go beyond hello to ask Julia about herself, to inquire about her kids, maybe to ask about how a single mother could raise such a large family on $7.50 an hour and no benefits in southern Connecticut. And then perhaps to go the extra mile and help her out.

All it would have taken was *one person*. One follower of Jesus Christ. How sobering that was. How contrary to God's will that no one helped.

Serving others' needs is a central pillar of the Christian faith. Jesus summarized this succinctly in the fifth beatitude. When He taught "Blessed are the merciful," He encouraged us to care about each other. To look out for one another. To be especially attentive when someone might be hurting.

Beyond this, His instruction was to *take action* when someone needs assistance. We know that because the Greek underlying the word *merciful* in verse 7 is best translated as an *active* compassion—a compassion that entails deeds, not just pity. In simplest terms, the merciful are those who care about others enough to help carry their burdens.

So how could Julia be alone while surrounded at work by Christians?

The answer largely has to do with the nature of the workplace. When we're with family, neighbors, or fellow church members, caring about people and lending a hand often comes naturally for many of us. But even the most committed Christian—a person who may genuinely embrace the notion of treating his job as a ministry—will have trouble maintaining a caring attitude in the workplace. It's not that he has never cared. He may have. It's not that he's unaware that mercy is a Christian virtue. He is. It's just that the pressures of the modern workplace have afflicted him with something called "compassion fatigue."

Allow me to tap for you some of the psychological research to explain this common ailment and to suggest how you can beat it.

## WHY DON'T I CARE ABOUT MY CO-WORKERS AND CUSTOMERS ANYMORE?

This is a well-worn question for workplace researchers. They've found that if you don't care as much about the people around you at work as you used to, you may suffer from the compassion fatigue just mentioned—a common stress that is a cousin of burnout. In simplest terms, it means just what the term implies: that you've grown tired of caring. You're depleted. You don't have anything left for anybody else.

The academic research tells us that a lot of things can contribute to this condition.[3] Some of these things are obvious; others may be a bit of a revelation. The top five symptoms are these:

1. Too many hours of work (researchers call this

"quantitative role overload." Most people call it "too much work to do.")

2. Working for an unpleasant boss (I told you some were obvious.)

3. Performing work that requires skills you don't currently have

4. Performing work that requires you to deal with other people's problems all day long

5. A mismatch of your values with the organization's values

Any red flags for you? Maybe several? Then read on, my friend.

What's interesting about this line of research is that although it derives from secular literature, it gives us tremendous insight into why many Christians struggle with caring about people at work. Take the first one—you may be working too many hours. According to the Economic Policy Institute, on average we're now working more than 120 hours longer per year than we were in 1979[4]—a full three weeks more per year! If you're contributing to this upward trend, beware. Too much work crowds out a person's willingness and ability to care about co-workers' and customers' needs. That's a bit of a no-brainer.

So is number two on the list: working for an unpleasant boss. As you may know, there's no shortage of this species in the jungle. One boss in San Francisco asked his secretary to go to a local bar and "beep him" if she saw someone he might be attracted to. Another sent his secretary out in a blizzard to get him lunch and then later commented that the weather was "unfit for human beings." Third place goes to the boss who demanded that a subordinate check his head for lice. Then he compelled her to buy and *apply* the appropriate medication for him! True stories. I can't make up stuff like this.[5]

It's hard to overstate the emotional drain that an unfair or overbearing boss can have on a subordinate. Every area of one's life—from work to family to personal time to sleep—can be adversely affected by him or her. It's no wonder, then, that such a situation creates compassion fatigue. It erodes our capacity to care about other people's problems, since we have too many of our own to worry about.

Numbers three and four on the list might be less obvious pitfalls, but the research conclusions are pretty clear. People who regularly perform duties beyond their comfort zone of capability and people who are constantly addressing other people's problems (e.g., nurses, social workers, pastors, customer service representatives) can easily become overwhelmed. A frequent consequence is callousness toward co-workers and customers.

Lastly, look at number five. It's a huge canker sore for Christians working in secular environments. Are you ever pressured or directed to perform a task that offends your values? Do you work in an environment where gossip, office politics, and backstabbing are the norm? Do you ever have to compromise your ethics to make a sale—or keep a friend? If such things are typical of where you work, you've probably experienced a mismatch between your values and the values of your corporate culture. And according to Christina Maslach, a leading academic authority on the subject, this mismatch may be the *primary* contributing factor to compassion fatigue.[6] When you swim against the current of the corporate culture on a daily basis, you are in jeopardy of becoming jaded, debilitated, and ultimately deaf to the concerns of others.

---

*If you don't care as much about the people around you as you should, you may suffer from what researchers call "compassion fatigue."*

---

The bottom line here is that any of these five factors can lead to compassion fatigue—the exhausting feeling that all of your emotional resources are used up. And once you're afflicted, say two decades worth of studies, what often follows is something called "depersonalization." In plain English, we begin to withdraw from the people around us. We reduce the frequency of our interaction with co-workers and customers. We have less tolerance for people and experience more moodiness and impatience. We become less merciful, even indifferent.

Sound familiar? Sorry to tell you, but there's even more bad news. The research further demonstrates that your workplace-induced depersonalization will also spill over into your family and other personal relationships.

So if you're asking yourself, *Why don't I care as much about my co-workers and my customers as I should?* it may be explained in part by going back through that five-item list and checking off the factors that apply to you. Are you doing too much? Are you constantly rushing from task to task? Are you regularly in over your head, undertaking work well beyond your expertise? Is it just your boss? Or is it the whole corporate culture shaping you into its secular, inhospitable image?

Whatever the reason(s), if you've grown tired of caring about the people around you at work, you need to address it. Don't wait. Your response *will* make a difference. You see, the Julia Toledos of this world are in almost every workplace. They are people with kids and aging parents, people with financial troubles, people with relationship problems, people barely keeping their physical or emotional health afloat. They are people of all socioeconomic classes, of all races, of both genders. Not everyone's trial is a life-or-death situation, of course, but each of these people needs the love of Christ shown to him or her in a tangible way.

That's where you and I come in. We believers stand in that gap, tithing our time and energy. That pleases God. "Blessed are the merciful," said His Son, "for they will be shown mercy." If you think that compassion fatigue may be a problem for you, it's time to seek a solution.

## OVERCOMING COMPASSION FATIGUE

Many of the same doctors (in one sense of the word) who have identified the causes of compassion fatigue have also tried to figure out a cure. One of their conclusions is that you should get away from work for a while. Now, you don't need a doctorate to reach that conclusion. It's common sense, right? If your batteries are low, you need to recharge them. But the question is, How long do they stay charged? For how long does the vacation alleviate your compassion fatigue? Here's where these studies become very helpful.

Does the relief last for years? No. Months? Uh-uh. Weeks? Closer. Try *days*. The research indicates that the beneficial effects of some respite from work will fade *very* quickly. In particular, our best estimates show that relief from compassion fatigue and job stress in general begin to wane *after a mere three days back at work*. By day twenty-one, whatever relief we experienced is expected to be gone completely![7] Not good news for someone trying to remain merciful.

So how about some other strategies? Besides time off, the other solutions advanced by business scholars generally revolve around addressing the causes of compassion fatigue listed earlier (e.g., reduce your workload, get another boss, get another job).[8] The problem with those approaches is that we have no real evidence that any of them actually works in the long-term either. Before we know it, the fatigue problems of the old situation may resurface in the new one. Square-one syndrome.

It's not hopeless, though. Often, it seems that Scripture goes where academic research cannot. This is a classic case. If you want a lasting solution for your compassion fatigue—if you want to overcome your weariness in caring about others—don't just look to vacations, to weekends, or to a new job to renew you. Look to God. We read in Isaiah that God "gives strength to the weary and increases the power of the weak. Even youths grow tired and weary, and young men stumble and fall; but those who hope in the Lord will renew their strength" (Isaiah 40:29–31).

It's a timeless message. Isaiah underscores a pervasive biblical theme. When you are fatigued, when you don't care, when you feel like you can't give any more than you've already given, stop and ask God for help. Don't try to do it alone. God has endless strength; you don't. *So ask Him for the sensitivity to care.* Do you really think that He'll deny that sort of request? Do you really think He'd send His Son to teach "Blessed are the merciful" and then ignore us when we ask for a more merciful heart?

He won't. The solution for compassion fatigue—the only solution whose effects will not fade after three days or three weeks—is to regularly tap into the power of the Holy Spirit. Pray regularly that He will work through you on the job. Pray daily for those around you at work. Pray that you'll continue to care about them. Pray for the discernment to identify their pain. And pray for the energy and the wisdom to attend to it.

That prayer doesn't take much time each morning. "Lord, help me to care about the people around me at work today. Give me a merciful heart." What was that? Four point eight seconds? At that rate, you may even find the time to pray that two or three times in your workday. Devote more time if you can, but a few sincere seconds, when practiced habitually, are really all that it takes. No fancy research conclusions. No large-sample studies or correlation tables. Just God's empowerment.

---

## The hallmark of a Christian is care.

---

That's not to say that the time off recommended by these studies is unnecessary, mind you. It's both deserved and healthy. (Let's give credit where it's really due, though. It was God Himself who came up with that innovation: "Six days you shall labor and do all of your work, but the seventh day is a Sabbath to the LORD your God. On it you shall not do any work" [Exodus 20:9–10].) But it is to say that a cure for compassion fatigue is available regardless of how many vacation days you have left.

The hallmark of a Christian is care. Mercy. Compassion. There's a lot at stake here—and not just for others. Without mercy, Christlikeness is impossible. With it, it's inevitable.

## Self-Check

---

Do you care about the people around you at work? Do you *really* care? If you don't, they'll know. We can't hide this for very long. It shows up in everything from the amount of time we invest in them, to our willingness to listen actively when they speak, to the way we say hello in the morning. When we're not genuine, it's transparent—and as people see through us, they seldom see Jesus Christ.

If you're struggling to be merciful at work, go back through that five-item list on pages 86–87. Try to address the items that might be stumbling blocks to your compassion. And, most of all, make time each workday to pray for a merciful heart and for the people around whom God has placed you.

## NOTES

1. John Koziol and Debra Estock, "Whistle at Night 'Unusual,'" *Fairfield Citizen-News*, 26 May 1999, p. 1.

2. "Friends Bemoan Fate's Cruel End to New Lives," *Connecticut Post*, 27 May 1999, sec. A, p. 15.

3. See, for example, Cynthia L. Cordes and Thomas W. Dougherty, "A Review and Integration of Research on Job Burnout," *Academy of Management Review* 18, no. 4 (1993): 621–36.

4. Lawrence Mishel, Jared Bernstein, and John Schmitt, *The State of Working America, 1998–99* (Ithaca, N.Y.: Economic Policy Institute and Cornell Univ. Press, 1999).

5. Chronicle Wire Services, "World's Worst Bosses," *San Francisco Chronicle*, 22 April 1991, sec. C, p. 3.

6. See Christina Maslach and Michael P. Leiter, *The Truth About Burnout* (San Francisco: Jossey-Bass, 1997), 55–59. See also Carol Smith, "Burnout Not Just a Personal Problem," *Sacramento Bee*, 11 January 1998, sec. D, p. 2.

7. Mina Westman and Dov Eden, "Effects of a Respite from Work on Burnout: Vacation Relief and Fade Out," *Journal of Applied Psychology* 82, no. 4 (1997): 516–27; and Dalia Etzion, Dov Eden, and Yael Lapidot, "Relief from Job Stressors and Burnout: Reserve Service as Respite," *Journal of Applied Psychology* 83, no. 4 (1998): 577–85.

8. See, for example, Maslach and Leiter, *The Truth About Burnout*, 61–101.

# Obstacle 6

# INGRATITUDE

*Blessed are the pure in heart,
for they will see God.*
MATTHEW 5:8

The kids had me at the end of my proverbial rope yet
again. It was a familiar position. I had been a regular
dangler ever since becoming a parent. So I raised my
voice for what seemed to be the hundredth time that
month trying, as usual, to get them to keep their pre-
cious little hands off of each other. Then I huffed out of
the house, muttering something about James Dobson
not being able to succeed with these kids. I just needed to get to my office where it was safe and solitary.

But no sooner did I get there than a colleague of
mine knocked on the door. *Not now,* I thought. *Can't
you see from my expression that I'm having an off day?
(More like an off life since I achieved dad status!)
Please take a hint and come back another time . . .*
She didn't. Instead she told me something that kicked
me square between the eyes, knocking some sense
into me to this very day.

"I need to talk to somebody. Yesterday my daughter was diagnosed with leukemia."

Her daughter was eight years old. And it wasn't the 97 percent cure-rate kind of leukemia. The chances were one in three that she wouldn't make it.

I'd like to report that I had comforting words for my friend, but quite frankly, I don't remember much else about the conversation. What remains vivid, though, was the aftershock in my life. Her news came on the heels of my own martyrdom. One moment I was feeling sorry for myself; the next, everything had changed. How foolish was my attitude toward my own kids. How selfish of me to think I had it so tough. How blind of me to not see all that I had been blessed with.

I sat at my desk that day too distracted to work effectively. I had to get home. I had to hug the kids and silently thank God for each one. When I finally walked through the door, lo and behold, they were fighting again. Angel Two had stolen the toy of Angel One and now One had Two pinned to the ground. But a fresh outlook insulated me from my typical exasperation. These kids were a blessing, not a burden. They were healthy. They were energetic. They were God's gift to me. That didn't mean their anarchy went unaddressed, mind you. I did, however, address it in a way that was closer to Jesus' persona than to my own.

Have you been there? Have you ever had an experience that immediately put everything in your life into a stark, new perspective? Have you lived through something that instantly inverted your mind-set from how little you had to how much you had? From how tough you had it to how much tougher it could be? And, if so, have you noticed how that new mind-set can radically change your attitude and behavior toward everyone around you?

Most of us, it's safe to say, have experienced such pivotal moments. God seems to furnish them regularly. A near-brush with death, a temporarily lost child at the mall, a middle-of-the-night phone call that fortunately turns out to be a wrong number, a narrow escape from the company's reduction-in-force. Such events bring almost all other concerns to a halt. They shine a brilliant light on what matters and what really doesn't. They have the power to turn us from counting our problems to counting our blessings. And, as we do, people notice a change in us.

How large a change? It depends. For those who already personify Christ daily, the change may be a small but welcome one. They've gone from the 90th to the 92d percentile on the sanctification index, so few in their circle might detect the results. For the less righteous, like the guy who had lost perspective regarding his kids, the change registers on the Richter scale.

At least for a while.

Have you been there? Have you ever experienced such a change? If so, *for how long?*

Unfortunately, these momentous events tend to kill off our old selves in the same way we futilely try to kill off a dandelion. The next day, there it is again! With the next crisis du jour, that old self is back. Same attitude, same behavior, same disappointing witness.

When that happens, we've missed an opportunity, an opportunity that comes directly from God. He's just tried to give us a ride on the Concorde to Christlikeness—even given us a taste of its destination—but we parachuted out at the first sign of turbulence.

My guess is that we wouldn't bail if we knew what the Pilot was up to. That's what this chapter is about. If you have the time, it might be worth your while to read it closely. And if you don't have the time, at least take this away with you: The difference between gloomy Moment One and joyous Moment Two can be summarized in one word: *gratitude.*

---

*Gratitude is the key to being pure in heart.*

---

Why did my perspective change regarding my kids? Gratitude. They didn't have any fatal diseases. Why do we celebrate life after the lab test reports that the lump is benign? Gratitude. Our worst fears are history. Why are we more satisfied with our jobs after dodging the layoff hatchet? Gratitude. I'm still employed and getting paid. In such cases, we realize what we've been taking for granted all along and recognize how much worse things could be. And curiously, we often find ourselves to be better people as a result. That's because gratitude is the key to being what Jesus called "pure in heart."

## THE SECRET TO PURITY OF HEART

"Blessed are the pure in heart" is, in fact, the heart of the Beatitudes. Many consider it to be a lesson that encompasses many of the others. But what exactly does it mean? As we look behind Jesus' words—actually, behind His quotation—we find out.

As with so many of His teachings, Jesus rooted His

instruction here in the Scriptures of His day, what we now call the Old Testament. For example, the concepts of being poor in spirit and comforting those who mourn come from Isaiah 61. The meek inheriting the earth comes from Psalm 37. Hungering and thirsting comes from Psalm 107. In a similar vein, the term *pure in heart* comes from Psalm 24:3–4. That passage illuminates what was in Jesus' mind when He said "pure in heart":

> Who may ascend the hill of the LORD? Who may stand in his holy place? He who has clean hands and a pure heart, who does not lift up his soul to an idol. (Psalm 24:3–4)

So again, if we ask, Who is pure in heart? it would appear from the context in the psalm that it is those people who never turn to idols. Piece of cake, right? I don't bow down before a stone pig displayed on a mantel. I don't worship the ocean or a forest or some satanic graven image. So I guess I'm not an "idol worshiper." By extension, then, I must be reasonably pure in heart, right?

Well, not exactly. Looking back for a moment to chapter 1, "Obstacle 1: Your Personal Golden Calf," we'll recall that idol worship entails putting any-thing—*anything*—ahead of God's will in our daily lives. Think about the enormous implications of that. Do you sometimes decide to make your own rules? To disregard God's inconvenient instruction? To treat people the way they "deserve" to be treated rather than the way God would have you treat them? To respond to conflict in a way that delivers both choice words and immediate gratification? To allow your thoughts to drift toward revenge, lust, or envy? Those kinds of commonplace actions also constitute idol worship, for when we engage in them, we are, in a biblical sense, making an idol out of *ourselves.* In other words, we are doing things our own way rather than God's way—putting our will first and God's will second. The Bible calls that *pride,* and according to Scripture, it is among the most egregious violations of God's law.

If you're struggling to buy into this interpretation of pure in heart, consider how consistently the Old and New Testaments define it. Specifically, look at James 4. After quoting a proverb on pride—"He [God] mocks proud mockers but gives grace to the humble" (Proverbs 3:34, quoted in James 4:6)—James said that a prideful attitude signifies an impure heart. "Wash your hands, you sinners," he followed in 4:8, *"and purify your hearts, you double-minded"* (italics added).

What does it mean to be pure in heart? James said that it was to avoid double-mindedness—to avoid being guided simultaneously by God's will and our own. This split personality, his context made clear, was the fruit of pride.

And it's not advisable, said James. Actually, being James, he was less delicate about it. A closer paraphrase might be: "You call yourself a believer? Then knock off the schizophrenia! Adopt a *single-minded* focus on God's will in everything you do. God should be at the beginning and the end of your relationships. He should be at the beginning and end of your decisions, large and small. In fact, you need to go beyond right actions. Your every thought should begin and end with the question 'What is God's will here?' This is what it means to be truly humble, to have no idols—to have a pure heart."

Given the term's implications, Jesus' words "Blessed are the pure in heart" are indeed problematic. If purity of heart really requires that level of God-centeredness—all the way down to our thought life—then who could possibly pass the test? Who could aspire to Jesus' lofty standard? Are the pure in heart ministers? Elders? Nuns in Calcutta? Monks in Nepal? Who exactly is "blessed" here? (One thing's for sure, it doesn't seem to be business professors!)

Many people are. In setting the bar this high, Jesus did not intend purity of heart to be a *destination* so much as a *direction*. No one except Jesus Himself has ever attained purity of heart by this definition. Nonetheless, we are all called to make an effort, to persist in the right direction, to work toward a God-centered existence as our primary objective in life.

Sound like a lot of work? It is. Sound like it's impossible? It's not. You can move closer to being pure in heart—you can be a better person to everyone around you this very day—if you focus on being thankful for the blessings in your life. Gratitude has the effect of draining our pride and purifying our heart. It cuts in half those of us who are double-minded.

Deep down, you probably know this to be true. In fact, you may be one of the legions of Christians who personally have seen this principle in its glorious operation. You may have already identified gratitude as the secret to a happy, God-honoring life and experienced its power in your home, your neighborhood, and your church.

. . . but then you go to work.

## THE OBSTACLE OF INGRATITUDE IN THE WORKPLACE—AND HOW TO OVERCOME IT

A funny thing happened after my disposition changed toward my kids. Nothing changed at work. I was the same "idol worshiping," disgruntled cog in my employer's wheel. Strange. Because of my new-found gratitude, I had become more Christlike at home, but that perspective somehow missed the bus to work each morning.

As I sat back and reflected on that phenomenon, I wondered why the principle of gratitude's leading to purity of heart didn't apply on company time. Then I realized: It can. Of course it can. It's a scriptural prin-ciple! Problem is, though, the way most people think about their jobs prevents them from tapping into the power of this principle. That is, our usual workplace mind-set encourages *ingratitude* on our part, there-by creating an obstacle to purity of heart.

Let me explain it this way. How many people have you ever met who are thankful for their work? I mean *genuinely* thankful? How many times have you come into work Monday morning to find someone—let's call him Herman—effervescing with gratitude for all he has in that job? Herman is thankful for being em-ployed. He's thankful for his five-by-five cubicle and his antiquated computer. He's thankful for his pay-check, his benefits, his phone line, the air-condition-ing, even for the stack of files on his desk. Herman is thankful that his garbage can was emptied last night! And, most especially, he's thankful for the privilege of working in a free country with unlimited opportuni-ties. Week in and week out, Herman's the happiest guy in the office.

I know what you're thinking. Drug test Herman immediately. Call security, march this guy down to the men's room, and send his sample off to the lab. Herman's one taco short of a combination plate.

Why would we think that about our friend? Simply because people just don't adopt that mind-set in the contemporary workplace. Let's face it; in our culture it's not normal to feel grateful for what we have at work. In fact, the whole notion of gratitude might seem misplaced in that context. Even a bit bizarre.

---

*In our culture, it's not normal to feel grateful for what we have at work.*

---

"Why should I be grateful for what I'm doing on this job?" we might ask. "I'm doing it for someone else! I'm slaving away for these people forty or fifty hours a week and for what? Yes, I get paid (and not enough!), but I *earn* it. I'm not going to thank anyone for what's owed to me. And as far as benefits or air-conditioning or garbage removal, well, every company offers that. No, I'm not the one who should be grateful in this place. It's the guys behind the desk who should be grateful to me. But I won't hold my breath for a 'thank-you' . . ."

Herman's a wacko. I'm realistic.

Perhaps. But chances are, Herman's got a significantly better shot at being pure in heart at work than do the realists. He's discovered the better path. He's broken free from the suffocating mind-set that chokes most of us on the job. He's the only one in his work environment who is choosing to concentrate on what he has rather than on what's missing. *It's a work mind-set that works miraculously.*

Are you searching for the power to finally become more like Jesus in your workplace? And would you like the invaluable added benefit of perpetual job satisfaction at the same time? Then consider taking some tips from Herman.

Inside his desk, Herman has a long list of the things that his work and his company offer him—things like pay and benefits, a safe workplace, a coffee machine, a refrigerator for his lunch, clean bathrooms, the opportunity to make friends—the list runs for three pages. Alongside it, he has another list—a list of all the things that could be worse in his job. He could have cutthroat co-workers; he could have Dilbert's boss; he could work in a hazardous occupation; his job security could be much worse . . . This list took longer to compile, but now it's almost as long as the first. He looks at both lists periodically and adds things he had forgotten earlier. It helps him to remain thankful.

Away from work, Herman does things like occasionally reading the obituaries or walking through a cemetery. Sounds creepy, but he finds that it reminds him of the brevity of life. Herman never watches casually when a news story comes on TV about tragedies like earthquakes, hurricanes, urban shoot-outs, or drownings. Instead, he pays close attention, looks into the eyes of the victims and their families, prays for them, and thanks God that he and his loved ones were not casualties.

On the lighter side, Herman sometimes likes to take out *The Guinness Book of World Records* and think about how much more difficult his life could be. It really helped put things in perspective one day when he learned that a guy named Charles Osborne is on record as having hiccuped from 1922 to 1990 and that Donna Griffiths began sneezing on January 13, 1981, and sneezed over 1 million times in the next twelve months.[1] For Herman, things might sometimes seem bad in his life, but they could sure be a lot worse!

Herman keeps in his wallet one statistic: If he had lived one hundred years ago, his life expectancy would have been forty-seven years.[2] He'd be gone by now! He also keeps one verse in there: "What do you have that you did not receive?" (1 Corinthians 4:7).

You see, Herman has disciplined himself into another way of thinking, both in and out of the workplace. He has made a habit of reminding himself daily just how blessed he really is. Gratitude has changed his life and made him far more pure in heart and far more content than he would have ever been otherwise. As a result, in many ways, Herman has "seen" God, as promised in the sixth beatitude.

Not face-to-face, of course. That'll come later. But he has seen God's power in his life. He has seen God speak through his lips. He has seen God transform him from an angry person into a model father, husband, co-worker, and friend. Herman has even seen God change other people through his now-infectious personality. No, Herman's not a wacko (and, for the record, he did pass his drug test). Quite the contrary. Herman is a living testimony to Jesus' promise: "Blessed are the pure in heart"—the ones who successfully embrace gratitude as a core life-philosophy—"for they will see God."

And as a result, countless others will see God through them.

## AN INVITATION TO CHANGE YOUR LIFE

Gratitude changes everything.

You can see that for yourself the next time you have one of those stop-you-in-your-tracks experiences—the kind described in the opening paragraphs of this chapter. In the midst of such an experience, please consider something. God may want to use that event to talk to you. He may be communicating something of life-changing proportions, showing you that gratitude is the fastest route to real contentment and to the perpetual purity of heart for which so many Christians hunger.

Listen for God's voice during that time. Seldom can we hear it more clearly.

Even better, listen for God's voice *today*. You don't have to wait for cancer tests or a late-night phone call to begin purifying your heart. You only need to make a choice—and then stick to it.

That second part will take some work, for sure, but most worthwhile things do. You'll have to develop a new habit—a habit of doing things to remind yourself how much God has bestowed upon you. It's a habit of thinking in terms of how much worse things could be. Whether you borrow Herman's techniques or invent your own, the reward will be the best life you could possibly live. Gratitude is the gateway to joy and faithfulness. Ingratitude is the primary obstacle to them.

That's a truth that applies both in the workplace and outside of it. As with all of the Beatitudes, Jesus' teaching on being pure in heart is a timeless, boundary-less principle. What this means for you as an employee, though, is that God's user-friendly formula—"Be thankful!"—is your ticket to more job satisfaction and a more consistent witness in the workplace.

Try getting those benefits from your human resources department!

## Self-Check

In a culture where so many of us have been blessed with so much, it's pretty natural to begin taking things for granted—and in doing so, to become discontented with our lives and less pure in heart. Have you lost sight of the blessings in your life? Have you drifted into a daily mind-set of ingratitude? Do you go to sleep at night or wake up in the morning thinking more about what you don't have than what you do have? Could this be affecting your ability to authentically live your faith?

Take some time to take inventory of all you have—and then take note of how quickly discontentment and impurities begin to drain away.

## NOTES

1. *The Guinness Book of World Records* (New York: Bantam, 1999), 171.

2. Center for Disease Control and Prevention/National Center for Health Statistics, *U.S. Decennial Life Tables, 1989–91* 1, no. 3 (1999): 10. This document is available at www.cdc.gov/nchswww/data/de89_1_3.pdf

# Obstacle 7

# BEING AN "EYE FOR AN EYE" GUY

*Blessed are the peacemakers, for*
*they will be called sons of God.*
MATTHEW 5:9

A friend of mine in the insurance business told me this story about a wacky claim they were handling. An elderly woman in a Cadillac was having trouble finding a parking space at the mall. All the close spots were taken, and many of the further spots were too small for the tank she was driving. After circling for about ten minutes, she finally lucked out. A minivan was pulling out near the mall entrance. Her timing was perfect. She put on her blinker and waited for them to leave.

You probably know what's coming. You've seen the scene. As soon as the van vacated, two kids in a sports car raced in, cutting off the woman in the process. The woman rolled down her window, keeping her temper in check, and politely told the boys that she had been waiting for the spot. So the driver said he was sorry and moved his car—yeah, right! Quite the opposite. The driver, freshly graduated from permit to license, offered up his seventeen-year-old middle digit and said: "In case you forgot, Granny, that's what it's like to be young and fast!"

Having enjoyed a laugh, he and the other choirboy proceeded to the mall entrance. Just as they got to the door, though, they heard a crash. Breaking glass, crunching metal, burning rubber. It sounded ugly. To their horror, they turned and found the front of Granny's Caddie buried deep into the trunk of their car. Then she backed up, put her car in drive and gunned it, ramming their car again!

One more for good measure? *Why not?* she thought. After all, the Corvette hadn't fully penetrated the brick wall in front of it yet. Reverse, drive, gas. It was *The Revenge of the Granny,* Parts 1, 2, and 3.

The young, fast teens ran to their car in a panic, unleashing a string of obscenities longer than their pending repair bill. But the woman remained unfazed. She calmly exited her car, approached the boys, and handed them a business card.

"Here's the number of my attorney," she said with a smug grin. "That's what it's like to be old and rich!"

Admit it. Deep down, if not further up as well, you're cheering. You can't hide the smile, so don't bother trying. Just let out what you want to say: "Yessssss! Way to kick butt, Granny! You go, girl!"

How can I be so sure that you liked that ending? Because I've been experimenting with this story. Told it to dozens of people. I've gotten more mileage out of this story than Granny did from her '84 Caddie. And almost invariably, the person listening to the story gets a satisfied look on his face as he learns how this woman responded. It's a look that says, "Good for her! Give those jerks what they deserve!"

Payback is fun. Settling the score satisfies. Revenge is rewarding. That's evident throughout our culture. Just look at what we find entertaining. One of the best parts of a hockey game is a fight. One player instigates. The other drops the gloves. Don't touch that remote. In baseball, the showstoppers are the bench-clearing brawls that ensue after a batter is hit by a pitch. The World Wrestling Federation, an entertainment company built on payback and pectorals, has become so popular that it's now gone public, offering stock on the NASDAQ. Hulk Hogan and Sergeant Slaughter are household names. Minnesota has even gone so far as to elect a professional wrestler, Jesse "The Body" Ventura, to its highest office! And then there's daytime TV. We regularly pause from channel surfing to watch the shouting match du jour on Jerry Springer. If that's not on, there's always a soap opera —perhaps the epitome of glorified retribution.

It's obvious from the Nielsen ratings that most of us like that kind of stuff. We have a penchant for payback. It's in our nature. That's further evidenced by a recent study. According to *American Demographics* magazine, 43 percent of respondents to a large survey indicated that if someone hurt a loved one, they would try to hurt them back. And another 41 percent said they weren't sure how they'd react. *That leaves only 16 percent responding that they're confident that they would not retaliate.*[1]

How about you? When the opportunity to retaliate comes your way, do you respond just like everyone else? You might not ram any cars, but do you take actions that look just the same to God? Do you repay "an eye for an eye," or do you turn the other cheek?

If you're more of an "eye for an eye" guy (or gal), consider taking a moment to sit on the mountainside. Find a flat surface and get comfortable. Judge Jesus has something to say about Granny's road rage —and our own.

## THE SAGE ON ROAD RAGE

Retaliation is both part of our fallen condition and continually reinforced by our environment. As a result, it's a potent temptation—and the same temptation that many on the Mount were struggling with.

Jesus knew that. He knew what was in their hearts. He knew their trials. He knew their history. Back in chapter 2, we talked a little bit about that history—a saga of hostile takeovers, cultural desecration, and ethnic cleansing. Not all the persecuted wallowed quietly in their despair, though. Many Israelite "zealots" actively sought to avenge the oppression of their people. They waited, and they planned. And when an opportunity presented itself, they would run their Caddies over as many Roman soldiers as possible.

To hear a zealot tell it, revenge would be bloody and sweet. God would work through the sword to deliver His people as He had in the past. God had done it that way with the judges. He had done it that way through King Saul and King David. Truly, those with the courage to fight for Israel's freedom would partake in this distinguished tradition, earning the title "sons of God."

And then with one sentence, Jesus turned that thinking on its head. Out of His mouth did not come "Blessed are the sword shakers" or "Blessed are the land takers" or "Blessed are the car breakers." He taught, "Blessed are the peacemakers." It is *they* who "will be called sons of God."

Can you hear the collective gasp of the revolutionaries? Barabbas probably headed for the parking lot early. He gave Granny a high five along the way. Back inside the stadium, Jesus was busy elaborating on His principle. "You have heard that it was said, 'Eye for eye, and tooth for tooth.' But I tell you, Do not resist an evil person. If someone strikes you on the right cheek, turn to him the other also. . . . Love your enemies and pray for those who persecute you, that you may be sons of your Father in heaven" (Matthew 5:38–39, 44–45).

The seventh beatitude is a lesson for those who are tempted to avenge an offense—both then and now. Those who are worthy of being called "sons of God" are not those who retaliate, but those who live peaceably with one another. A counterstrike is not God's answer. Love and forgiveness are.

It's an uncomfortable lesson for those of us who are more gifted in conflict escalation than conflict resolution. But penchant for payback or not, Jesus says, "Put down your sword. Respect God's yield sign. Turn the wheel and go search for another parking spot."

## PAYBACK WHILE EARNING A PAYCHECK

And if you think that's a tough lesson to follow at the mall, try it at work. In no place is it easier or more tempting to retaliate. Think about it. If you wanted to get even with somebody at work—and do it covertly —would that be difficult for you? Probably not. It might take a little creativity and some planning, but anybody could pull it off. That's because we work in environments where almost everybody is vulnerable to everyone else. On the job, revenge isn't just sweet, it's *available*.

And as a result, it's widespread. I recently stumbled across a Web site that essentially serves as a bulletin board for people to post stories of getting even in the workplace.[2] The public commentary is voluminous. A few of the posted escapades amount to mere pranks. Most, though, are costly and a bit depraved. In addition to the time-honored techniques of pulling fire alarms and vandalizing cars, the more imaginative vigilante justice these days includes

- Waving powerful magnets near computers, thereby erasing all of the memory
- Changing all of the computer screens to black characters on a black background (how long did it take the victim to diagnose *that* problem?)
- Throwing back miniscule tips at customers as they exit a restaurant
- Dialing a 1-900 number from a co-worker's phone after work hours and then leaving the phone off the hook all night ($8.95 a minute; must be at least eighteen to call)
- Giving sensitive information on pricing to a competitor
- Submitting subscription cards with a co-worker's name and address to hundreds of magazines
- Sending a package of "returned" lingerie to a male co-worker's house with a good-bye note from a fictional mistress—and sending the pack-

age by taxi at a time when only his wife was
home to receive it

There are dozens more, but you get the idea. If you
want to get back at somebody at work, there are
countless options at your disposal. Expensive options. Destructive options. Even quick verbal options— something like repaying insult for insult. The
only question is whether you will exercise any of
them.

For many of us, it's hard not to. At the emotional
moment of decision, we have two powerful forces
pushing us toward reprisal. First, there's our *desire* to
strike back, courtesy of our sinful nature. Something
inside of us just makes us want to do it. Then, as we've
just seen, there's the abundant *opportunity* to strike
back, courtesy of our mutual vulnerability in the
workplace.

Desire times opportunity. It's a lethal formula
whose product is the temptation to retaliate.

---

*Desire x Opportunity =
Temptation to Retaliate*

---

Now, temptation is not sin. Hebrews 4:15 says that
even our sinless Savior experienced temptation ("For
we do not have a high priest who is unable to sympa-
thize with our weaknesses, but we have one who has
been tempted in every way, just as we are—yet was

without sin"). But giving in to that temptation is sin. So to avoid acting on your temptation to retaliate, you need to attack temptation on both the desire and the opportunity front. Let me take "opportunity" first, since that's the easier one.

Without opportunity, you cannot act in vengeance. The workplace misdemeanors listed above would not have occurred absent an open door to perform them. A person leaves her cubicle unguarded. Exiting customers hang around for a few minutes after leaving fifty cents on the table. Files containing classified information remain generally accessible. It's almost too easy.

The solution here is to *run*. At the moment of temptation, run from the situation immediately. The longer you stay while opportunity knocks, the more likely you are to open the door. So run as far and as fast as you can away from that door. The clearest biblical example of this comes from its first book, Genesis. A young man, sold into slavery by his brothers, was being propositioned by the Egyptian governor's wife. The opportunity was there, practically screaming at him to submit. It was a temptation. But Joseph ran from Potiphar's wife and, in doing so, avoided acting on that temptation (see Genesis 39).

In the same way, when you are presented with the opportunity to get even with a co-worker (or anyone for that matter), *run*. Do whatever it takes. If the opportunity is zero, temptation will be zero (you math jocks can verify that using the formula).

From *desire*, though, we can't run because no matter where we run to, there we are! Still desirous. Still craving payback. Still seeking to return and create an opportunity. Running from temptation is an important first step, but it may not be enough since we could end up running right back. Granny could have driven away from her golden opportunity, but after a few simmering laps, she might have returned to squash the Vette anyway.

How do you prevent this? How do you extinguish a flaming desire to get even? What could Granny do while driving those laps?

The same thing that you and I could do after we've initially run from a tempting situation. We can work to forgive the offender. To give up the right to be mad at him. To completely clear his slate. To drop it altogether. "For if you forgive men when they sin against you, your heavenly Father will also forgive you," Jesus said in His sermon (Matthew 6:14). This is the path to being a "peacemaker"—to being a son of God.

And as you probably know, it's also the toughest path you'll ever have to walk. Jesus knew that about us too. Maybe that's why He instructed us to "pray for those who persecute you" (Matthew 5:44). Have you ever tried that? It's painful at first, but if you can stick with it, it becomes a surprisingly liberating experience. It drains our desire to strike back since it's virtually impossible to remain mad at someone for whom you are praying. That opens a different door—the door to forgiveness—and double-locks the door to revenge.

Trust me on this one. Try this approach the next time you're feeling the pull of temptation. I know; praying for your persecutor is the last thing you want to do, but try it anyway. Just once. The only things you have to lose are your anger, your hatred, and your desire to get revenge.

We can summarize all of this with another equation, one derived by none other than the Creator of mathematics Himself. Run + pray + work to forgive. It's a powerful formula that will keep both your desire and opportunities under control. And when you've mastered that math problem, you'll find that the sum is 0 percent temptation, 100 percent "son of God."

### REWINDING *THE REVENGE OF THE GRANNY*

"In case you forgot, Granny, that's what it's like to be young and fast!" Having enjoyed a laugh, he and the other choirboy proceeded to the mall entrance.

Granny wasn't happy about it, that's for sure. Thoughts of turning that Vette into an accordion danced through her head. She had the money to do it with impunity. But then she thought better of it. "Blessed are the peacemakers," she recalled from her Bible study. Blessed are those who can overlook an offense, who can forgive, who can choose the path of reconciliation over retaliation. She continued down the row, silently praying that the boys would come to know Jesus Christ and that their lives would be transformed.

OK, that ending isn't nearly as exciting, right? No crunching metal? No piercing one-liners? It would never play in Hollywood. It would never air on Springer. And if I had told the story that way to my friends, I suspect that most of them would have wondered why I was wasting their time. It's a disappointing ending.

. . . except to God.

## Self-Check

We live in an "eye for an eye" world. That's the norm. The question you might want to ask yourself, then, is "Am I normal?" Are you like so many others when it comes to retaliation, or are you more like Jesus?

You can better gauge this by looking at your track record. When was the last time you really forgave someone despite a strong temptation to retaliate? Was it recently, or has it been quite a while? If it's the latter, that might be a red flag.

Consider being "abnormal" today and see what God does with that decision. Take steps to improve some of your relationships by choosing God's path of peacemaking.

### NOTES

1. Bernice Kanner, "Turning the Other Cheek," *American Demographics* 20, no. 2 (1998): 39.

2. Http://www.disgruntled.com/even.html

# Obstacle 8

# PEOPLE-PLEASING

*Blessed are those who are persecuted because
of righteousness, for theirs is the kingdom of
heaven. Blessed are you when people insult
you, persecute you and falsely say all kinds of
evil against you because of me. Rejoice and
be glad, for great is your reward in heaven.*
MATTHEW 5:10–12

What if the story went something like this?

Saul wasn't exactly the kind of guy you'd invite to
your weekly Bible study. If you did, it might be your
last. But one day on the road to Damascus, he saw the
light and did a complete 180, becoming a disciple of
Jesus Christ. He went from terrorist to activist practically overnight. His new mission: Convert the Gentiles.

To increase his chances of success, he started by
adopting the Greek name Paul. Then one of his first
stops was Galatia—lots of theological confusion there.
So Paul took a crack at setting them straight.

Some in Galatia thought that they had to be cir-
cumcised to be right with God. Some thought they
had to keep the whole Law to gain His favor. Many

thought they had to do both. Still others said it was
neither. And to make matters worse, these four Gala-
tian camps were really entrenched in their positions.
That worried Paul. If he came down too firmly on one
side or the other, he'd offend some people. But God
commanded Paul to give them the truth, so he tabled
his concerns about friendship and sided with the far-
left camp, preaching that salvation was by grace
through faith alone. No need to cut yourself. No need
to be slaves to the Law. It could only condemn you
anyway.

Paul's poll numbers immediately plummeted. His
critics pounced on him during the next round of Sunday talk shows, claiming that Paul was preaching a
gospel of cheap grace. Worse yet, he was turning
Christianity into a catalyst for sin. "The guy," one re-
porter said on CNN, "no doubt flunked out of the
Jerusalem church—and now he's spewing his heresy
to whoever will listen!"

*I knew it,* Paul thought. *I wanted so badly to make
a good impression, but now I've blown it. Maybe it's
not too late.* Then Paul got inclusive. "Actually, guys,
you might be right," he backpedaled. "There's room
for all of us under God's big tent. Maybe you can work
your way into heaven and maybe you can't. Only God
knows for sure." After that, they all liked Paul and respected his willingness to tolerate different view-
points.

Some time later, Paul visited the city of Thessalonica, a big government town that would put Wash-
ington, D.C., to shame. I mean, these folks went so far
as to erect a statue and a temple to the honor of Julius
Caesar. They even worshiped someone named Zeus,

whom they called the father of all the gods. Zeus had his own statue down the road in Olympia.

Anyway, Paul, along with his sidekicks Silas and Timothy, surmised that this, too, was fertile ground for evangelism. So Paul preached in the synagogue on three consecutive Sabbaths, spreading the good news of the suffering Messiah and His resurrection.

But the Thessalonians built no statue in Paul's honor. Instead, they wanted to bury him beneath one. *Not again!* Paul lamented. *I* really *wanted these people to like me.* So he retracted his story on the next Sabbath. "What I meant to say," he clarified, "is that Jesus is really *Zeus'* son. And you know that old adage, 'Give to Caesar what belongs to Caesar'? Well, *Jesus is the One who coined it!* Doesn't get any more pro-government than that, huh, folks?"

Unfortunately for Paul, that didn't get him off the hook. The Thessalonians threatened to charge him with treason, since he was still suggesting that they bow down before someone other than Caesar. "No need to do that!" the alarmed apostle responded, anxious to avoid jail. "You guys are probably right. That Damascus Road thing was probably just a hallucination on my part. Bad wine, I guess. I'll be on my way now." After that, they all liked Paul, and he promised to write them soon.

Eventually, Paul needed some respite from the rough rhetoric, so he traveled to Corinth, the Las Vegas of the Greek world. Gambling, legalized prostitution, Budweiser on tap everywhere—these people knew how to party. Once there, though, Paul couldn't constrain himself from preaching, and, to his surprise, some of the high rollers actually bet his message was right. So Paul hung out in Corinth for an entire year and a half.

After he left, though, Paul was told that his new Corinthian brothers and sisters had become a bit full of themselves. Adopting the name *spirit-people*, they placed themselves somewhere below God but above men. And with this new privileged status, they went back to their old ways of sexual deviance. "Everything is permissible for us," they reasoned, "as it is for other spirit-people."

To underscore this belief, they even bragged about their lenience with a church member who was sleeping with his stepmother! Predictably, some in their number eventually began taking swipes at Paul himself, calling him arrogant, a wimp, and a bully.

What's a preacher to do? Paul's ministry of making friends was in serious jeopardy once again. Yes, the Corinthian believers were twisting the gospel. Yes, they were again indistinguishable from their pagan neighbors. But, hey, these were the 50s. *Perhaps I should get with the times,* Paul thought. *People should feel free to do their own thing.* So he sent them an enthusiastic letter telling them to keep up the good work. After that, they liked Paul very much.

Similar story in Rome, except this time Paul wrote them before visiting, taking it from the top with his theology. Some in the government, though, were outraged by Paul's message, so upon his arrival they threatened to throw him in jail and kill him. Paul did a quick cost-benefit analysis and decided to rip up the letter before hundreds of people—told them it was a forgery. Then he said good-bye to his Roman friends and sailed to the coast of Spain where he retired, kept quiet about his faith, and met lots more people who liked him very much.

## PEOPLE-PLEASING VERSUS GOD-PLEASING

What if the story went something like that? What if Paul elected to be a people-pleaser rather than a God-pleaser? What if his primary concerns as a witness were getting along with people, not offending anyone, and minimizing confrontation? What if he had tempered his message—God's message—so that he could avoid persecution?

Well, for starters, God probably would have raised up someone else to write the Epistles. Paul would be an obscure biblical footnote, having lived a life of little eternal impact. On a personal level, as well, Paul's development as a Christian would probably have been unimpressive. As we'll see in this chapter, persecution has a way of fast-tracking one's sanctification. People-pleasing reverses it.

Fortunately, though, like so many in the Bible, Paul chose God-pleasing over people-pleasing. His first and only allegiance was to Jesus Christ. This mindset he summed up succinctly to the Galatians: "Am I now trying to win the approval of men, or of God? . . . If I were still trying to please men, I would not be a servant of Christ" (Galatians 1:10). For Paul, it was one way or the other. We choose whether God's or man's evaluation comes first. We can't have it both ways: Serving Jesus Christ means putting Him first and not worrying about what people think of that.

Often, that will win you friends and build relationships as you imitate Christ by serving others. Sometimes, though, in a world increasingly hostile to the truth, it will lead to some form of persecution. Indeed, for his God-pleasing approach, Paul made many beloved friends, but he was also vilified in Galatia, run out of Thessalonica, ridiculed at Corinth, and jailed and—we think—ultimately killed in Rome.

---

*People-pleasing prevents persecution.
God-pleasing often leads to it.*

---

He could have avoided all of that had he been a people-pleaser. Many of us know this from personal experience: *People-pleasing prevents persecution. God-pleasing often leads to it.* So, fearing persecution, we typically choose the former over the latter. But one thing many Christians don't seem to embrace is that, as difficult as it is, persecution may be part of God's design for their lives. In fact, in our moments of persecution, we are called "blessed," according to the One Paul sought to please. "Blessed are those who are persecuted because of righteousness," Jesus assured us, "for theirs is the kingdom of heaven" (Matthew 5:10).

### PERSECUTION? A BLESSING?

It sounds a little convoluted—almost like a transparent sales pitch that tries to turn a liability into an asset.

"Sure, this beauty doesn't have air-conditioning," says the used-car dealer, "but think of the gas money you'll save as a result!"

"It's OK that you failed the exam," says the teacher. "We *learn* by failing."

"I know liver tastes bad," says your mother, "but it's *good for you.*"

For most of us, any kind of persecution is worse than liver. And when we're under attack, it's hard to see how this could possibly be "good for us." Since no one wants to be mistreated, and since Jesus offered seven less painful avenues to blessedness before He ever got to persecution, you may find yourself tempted to write off the value of persecution, jump to the epilogue, and close out this book.

If that's the case, please consider two brief points before you go. First, like Paul (and Noah and David and Isaiah and Daniel and John the Baptist and Jesus and the apostles and countless believers over the past two thousand years), we often encounter persecution by *God's design*. That is, God may intend for certain trials to visit us.

If I'm sounding a bit like that used-car salesman, let me defer to my Boss's policy manual.

Scripture tells us that committed Christians will run into resistance. John, for example, stated plainly, "Do not be surprised, my brothers, if the world hates you" (1 John 3:13). *Hates you.* That's strong language, and it's an echo from his Gospel, where he quotes Jesus as saying, "If you belonged to the world, it would love you as its own. As it is, you do not belong to the world. . . . That is why the world hates you" (John 15:19).

*Hates you.* Even stronger language is the Greek word that underlies Jesus' prophecy: *miseo.* The word connotes an active hatred—that is, a hatred that is not content to remain inside of a person. It is a hatred that culminates in external action, namely, persecution. It's no wonder, then, that Jesus continued His warning: "Remember the words I spoke to you: 'No servant is greater than his master.' If they persecuted me, they will persecute you also" (John 15:20).

His point is hard to miss. When you openly and intentionally follow in My footsteps, you *will* experience persecution. It's a restatement of what He had already taught them: People will "insult you, persecute you and falsely say all kinds of evil against you because of me" (Matthew 5:11). So expect it. Brace yourself for it. "Don't be surprised" by it. *Persecution in some form or another is a thermometer of Christian commitment.*

It's also a thermostat. This is point two. Persecution is a vehicle God uses to transform us from lukewarm to red-hot followers. Here's where the blessings from Matthew 5:10–11 come in. You might ask, "How is it a blessing when someone is gossiping about me? How is it a blessing when my job is threatened because of my faith? Why doesn't God bless me instead by FedExing a lightning bolt to this atheist who's using me as a verbal punching bag?" Perhaps because such trials have the capacity to make us stronger, to ratchet up our commitment, to make us more Christlike.

Again from that same policy manual, a well-worn passage on this point for Christians in the line of fire is James 1:2–4. In his typical cut-to-the-chase fashion, James didn't waste a second in tackling one of the toughest of theological issues. He wrote, regarding persecution:

> Consider it pure joy, my brothers, whenever you face
> trials of many kinds, because you know that the testing
> of your faith develops perseverance. Perseverance must
> finish its work so that you may be mature and complete,
> not lacking anything.

. . . Just like the One we follow was not lacking in
anything. James's message here is that persecution is
the expressway to Christlikeness. That's how he could
have the audacity to call our trials "pure joy." Persecution thickens our skin—over time, it may even ar-
mor plate it. It bolsters our ability to handle future
assaults. We develop "perseverance," James said—an
ability to endure opposition and trust in God as Jesus
did. We reach that elusive next level of "maturity and
completion" that would probably have remained
only a lofty goal had we not been persecuted. That's
how persecution can be a blessing.

---

*Persecution is the expressway
to Christlikeness.*

---

What all this means, then, is that when someone
wrongs you because of your faith, you should try to
take heart. Nothing sanctifies you more quickly. See
persecution for what it is—part of God's design, part
of His plan to reinforce us. There's no need to run
from it. There's no need to become a people-pleaser

to avoid it. There's no need to retaliate against or despise the person harassing you. In fact, you may even find some satisfying humor in his or her behavior, for those who persecute you because of your beliefs are unwittingly doing God's work! Without knowing it, they are operating as God's agents to strengthen and mature those who love Him. How's that for God's turning the tables?

I'm not sure I'd share that little nugget with your oppressor, but in the midst of persecution, it surely is a comforting irony, don't you think?

## THE PRESSURE TO BE A PEOPLE-PLEASER IN THE WORKPLACE

Then there's the workplace. Elsewhere, we may be able to overcome our fear of persecution and make the transition from people-pleaser to God-pleaser. But, as most 9-to-5ers know, the secular workplace presents a unique challenge. There, we confront built-in head winds every day—significant *job consequences* and *social consequences*—that continually threaten to blow us back to a people-pleasing mindset. Allow me two brief stories to illustrate this point.

Ken Roberts was a fifth-grade schoolteacher at Berkley Gardens Elementary School in Denver. As part of his reading curriculum, Ken assigned his students to read silently at their desks for fifteen minutes per day. The students could choose their own reading material, whether from home, from the school library, or from Ken's personal classroom library.

To set an example for the students, Ken also read silently during this reading period, frequently choosing to read the Bible he kept on his desk. Ken never read the Bible aloud to the students, nor did he ever proselytize them in any way. He simply wanted to tap into God's Word in his free moments on the job.

In 1986, Principal Kathleen Magadan twice noticed Ken at his desk with Bible in hand. On both occasions, she admonished him to cease this subversive activity. He could bring his Bible to work, but it was to remain in his desk during the *entire* school day. No exceptions.

Ken complied, but the tension didn't end there. The next year, after a parent-teacher open house, a parent complained to Principal Magadan that there were two Christian-oriented books among the 239 books in Ken's classroom library. The principal promptly ordered Ken to remove them. Again, Ken complied but asked to discuss the matter further at a later date. A few weeks and a few pleas down the road, Ken's appeal met with a restatement of the order—this time in writing: "Failure to comply with this directive will be considered insubordination and could result in disciplinary action."

Not exactly a veiled threat. This was quite explicit: Remove the books and don't read the Bible at your desk, or we'll use more persuasive means to address this problem.

Could the principal get away with that? Could she go so far as to prohibit Ken from reading Scripture silently at his desk? These days, it shouldn't be surprising that a court of law said yes. In the case of *Ken Roberts v. Kathleen Magadan*, this was the court's conclusion: "The school district acted for the valid purpose of preventing (Ken Roberts) from promoting Christianity in a public school."[1]

As Ken learned, overt expressions of faith—even innocuous ones like his—can have significant job consequences (effects on pay, promotion, scheduling, job security, relations with your boss). And it's not that rare. In my line of work, I regularly hear about cases like this one and I've used many of them in my classroom.

Before long, though, I found myself actually living one myself!

Early in my academic life, and in response to what I thought was God's will for my career, I made an abrupt shift from doing mainstream management research (i.e., performing secularized studies and publishing the results in obscure, erudite journals) to doing Bible-based management research (i.e., researching God's Word for His guidance on workplace issues and publishing the results in book form). And I was struck by how things can fall into place when you say yes to God. Publishers were responding enthusiastically. Radio shows were calling. Speaking opportunities opened up. Newspaper columnists visited my office. It was, to say the least, an exciting time for me.

A colleague of mine—let's call her Lisa—was excited too: excited at the potential to get rid of me!

I was oblivious to Lisa's behind-the-scenes activities until a friend from the next office stopped by and closed my door. "You need to know something," she said to this naive, untenured father of three. "Someone very influential is going door-to-door telling people to write negative letters when you come up for tenure."

Those of you in the teaching profession know

what was at stake. If someone does not receive tenure, he is fired. Gone. Pink-slipped. Yesterday's news. It's a bizarre (and nerve-racking), all-or-nothing moment when one is either given lifetime job security or put out onto the street. Lisa, therefore, was doing something that would not only short-circuit my career but could threaten the well-being of my family too.

I asked my friend, who had herself been visited by my nemesis, what Lisa's concern was. The response caught me off guard: I had become Ken Roberts!

"Mike is doing research that clearly is not appropriate for a business school," Lisa claimed. "Christianity has no place in our curriculum, in our research program, or in the business world."

I had a right to be angry, I thought. I had a right to protest to the dean. And I had a right to confront Lisa about this. But fortunately, God is wiser and conferred on me an inner peace about the situation. By the time my friend had finished debriefing me on this anonymous, "very influential" person's activities, I didn't even want to know the assailant's name. I simply thanked my friend for her concern and told her not to worry about it.

A year later, the tenure decision went my way. The damage was done, though. Lisa, although unsuccessful in exterminating this pest, had sufficiently poisoned the environment so that several of my colleagues now considered me an oddity—even a bit quirky. Many had lost respect for me. Some wondered aloud (to others) why someone with real potential would give it all up for that anti-intellectual religious stuff. On the tougher side, a few repeatedly made jokes about my work. Two colleagues even stopped talking

to me altogether. It had indeed become a more exciting time than I'd bargained for!

---

*Fear of persecution leads us to
be people-pleasers rather than
God-pleasers in the workplace.*

---

Now here's the point of these illustrations. Persecution comes to workplace Christians, and it comes
in many varieties. And on the job, it's seldom without
consequence. In both my case and Ken Roberts's
case, there were, first of all, potential *job consequences*
accompanying our expressions of faith. We could
have easily met on the unemployment line had we
lived in the same state. Beyond that, my particular
case included significant *social consequences* as well.
When people know that you are a follower of Jesus
Christ—and that you take that seriously—some may
go out of their way to harm you. It's a two-thousand-
year-old tradition. And let me tell you firsthand that
it makes for a really uncomfortable situation at work.
Each time I walked past someone who was no longer
speaking to me, it bothered me. Each time my former
friends neglected to invite me to lunch with them, it
annoyed me. Each time I had reached some mile-
stone to receive virtually no congratulations from my
peers, it frustrated me.

Perhaps you've felt similar discomfort. We all want
to be liked, accepted, and respected by those around

us in the workplace—both for job-related and social reasons. So one of the worst things that can happen to us, we reason, is to stand out as different and to risk the mistreatment at the hands of our boss or peers. *And it is precisely this fear of persecution that leads us to be people-pleasers rather than God-pleasers in the workplace.*

Does that resonate with you? Have you felt the extraordinary pull toward pleasing people in your work environment? If you want to really understand how to overcome this, dig a little deeper with me on this point.

## WHAT WORKPLACE RESEARCHERS HAVE LEARNED ABOUT PEOPLE-PLEASING

Interestingly, organizational psychologists have investigated our tendency toward people-pleasing, reaching conclusions that are helpful to workplace Christians. Of course, these Ph.D.'s don't use the term *people-pleasing.* Too blue-collar. Instead, the more polished vernacular is *impression management:* "the behaviors individuals employ to protect their self-image and influence the way they are perceived by significant others."[2] When you strip away the jargon and the complex sentence structures, though, it's the same thing.

The best available research on impression management nicely supplements our common sense on the matter. Although not everyone does this, most of us throughout our careers instinctively try to influence (1) how much people like us and (2) how much they will perceive that we are similar to them. You've played this game to some extent, haven't you? We do things like agree with people even though we don't really agree with them, do favors for higher-ups that go well beyond what we want to do for them, subtly flatter people, smile when we don't feel like it, use false modesty. It's our public face, and it's blemish-free.

Additionally, we want our co-workers to think that we fit in well here—that we are very much like them. Having others perceive us as similar to them is one of the most effective ways to gain their friendship. (For those of you who like scientific evidence, this is one of the most consistent findings in the impression management literature.) If we come off as having similar tastes, similar attitudes, and similar world-views, people will like us more. That outcome's naturally attractive to us. So whether we're conscious of it or not, we tend to do things to bring about that result. In doing so, we gain friends and sidestep some of the *social consequences* of being different.

According to the research, we also sidestep the *job consequences* by managing our boss's impression of us. These studies tell us that something very valuable accrues to people who skillfully navigate the impression-management game: They will likely receive better performance evaluations. There's a prize for those who play ball! If we say and do things that signal to the boss that we are similar to him and that we fit the model of the ideal employee, the research shows that we can affect things like the amount of work he gives us, the type of assignments we receive, the budget he allots for our work, and his willingness to accommodate our schedule.

Not enough goodies for you? Try some of this candy: If you manage your boss's perceptions well, come performance review time, there's a tendency for your boss to selectively recall your positive work behaviors while disregarding the things you didn't do so well. No wonder we're so tempted to play this game. We can possibly affect pay and promotion decisions through people-pleasing!

So impression management can be a powerful tool for anyone trying to get ahead. But stop and think for a moment what that may imply about the person who *refuses* to play that game—the one who *refuses* to be a people-pleaser. In particular, what happens when you step out of the mainstream in a secular workplace by admitting that your faith is important to you and that it affects the decisions you make, the way you work, and all your priorities in life?

That might seem pretty benign on the surface. In many work environments, though, it's anything but. Once you "rebel" in this way, you've communicated that you are not similar to everyone else—everyone who keeps faith issues private and never talks about them in the workplace. As a result, the impression-management effects operate in reverse. That doesn't mean that you'll have no friends or that the boss will hate you, only that you are more likely to run into those adverse job and social consequences described in the two cases earlier. In some workplaces, you may even experience *significant* persecution, anything from missing a promotion to the business equivalent of capital punishment: being fired.

Such is the nature of living as a God-pleaser. It's risky, and it always has been.

In the workplace, then, we have to make what

seems to be a hard choice. But take it from someone who's been there: It's not really that hard a choice to make or to stick with. If you recognize and consciously resist the pressures to please people rather than God, and if you remember that persecution can be a blessing, you will overcome a mountainous obstacle to Christlikeness in the contemporary workplace.

## UNWRAPPING GOD'S GIFT

Let's come back full circle to that independent contractor, Paul. What if, as he moved from job site to job site, he decided to avoid persecution by adopting a people-pleasing mind-set? What if he sold out the truth in order to duck confrontation, jail time, and beatings? *(And what if we did the same?)*

For one thing, those hearing Paul's words would have suffered, having been denied access to the good news of the gospel. None of them would have been able to tap the power of the gospel because Paul would have been too preoccupied with his image to plug them in. *(Some of the people around us every day at work might never hear the truth.)*

For another, Paul the people-pleaser would have lost out on something too—not his salvation, but his sanctification. By avoiding persecution, Paul would have deprived himself of God's continuing work in him through the Holy Spirit. His maturity in Christ would have stalled at Damascus. *(Have you checked your engine lately?)*

But Paul rejected people-pleasing, choosing instead to risk persecution. His experience and his words underscore two lessons covered in this chapter. First, Paul said, persecution is *inevitable* for the committed Christian: "In fact, everyone who wants to live a godly life in Christ Jesus will be persecuted" (2 Timothy 3:12). Anticipate it. It's an indicator that your eyes really are fixed on Christ.

Second, persecution can be a blessing because it helps grow us toward Christlike character: "We also rejoice in our sufferings, because we know that suffering produces perseverance; perseverance, character; and character, hope" (Romans 5:3).

If this latter verse is old terrain for you, as it is for many believers, try not to let its familiarity dilute its strength. Paul, as a God-pleaser, reminded us of both James's insight and of what Jesus taught on the Mount decades earlier: "Blessed are those who are persecuted because of righteousness. . . . Blessed are you when people . . . persecute you . . . because of me" (Matthew 5:10–11). They will, as a result, become more perseverant, more resistant to the world's temptations, more like the Master.

Notice one other thing about Romans 5:3, if you would—something you may never have thought of before. The sequence begins with suffering and ends with hope. Does that ring a bell? Actually, it almost amounts to plagiarism (but I'm sure the original Author didn't mind). You see, this is the exact journey Jesus mapped out at the end of the Beatitudes. Matthew 5:10–11 talks of our suffering (persecution), and verse 12 confers the hope: "Rejoice and be glad, because great is your reward in heaven."

Tell me something. Was it just by coincidence that "plagiarizer" Paul said we are to "rejoice" in our sufferings? Probably not. He was echoing Jesus' lesson that we will enjoy a better life if we can see our circumstances as God sees them.

And in many ways, that notion captures a primary purpose of the Beatitudes. God has gift wrapped for you a better life both today and tomorrow. All you have to do is open it. He says from the outset that your share in "the kingdom of heaven" is what's inside. Your task is to pull the ribbons of the Beatitudes—to begin seeing the world as He sees it—to access that gift.

Persecution may be the hardest ribbon of all for you to pull. But that's made easier if you can conquer the obstacle of people-pleasing and make yourself vulnerable to whatever persecution God may want to use in your life. As you do, you will find, like Paul, that the gift far exceeds any temporary discomfort of persecution. Inside the box is a more Christlike character and fulfillment beyond anything you've yet experienced.

Whatever the cost, no gift will ever be more rewarding for you to unwrap.

## Self-Check

Here's a powerful self-diagnostic exercise: Over the next twenty-four hours, pay close attention to how you think. In particular, take note of how many times you feel concerned about what someone else thinks of you. Do this at work, at the store, in your neighborhood, at home. Do it while you're getting dressed, looking into the mirror, driving, having conversations . . . you get the idea. Tally up your people-pleasing score, just for one day. Then ask yourself: "Might I be overly concerned with how others see me? Am I worrying too much about what others might think if they knew I take my faith seriously?" And on the more proactive side, "What can I do in the next twenty-four hours to be more of a God-pleaser than a people-pleaser?"

## NOTES

1. *Kenneth Roberts v Kathleen Magadan and Adams County School District No. 50,* 921 F.2d 1047, at 1059.

2. Sandy J. Wayne and Robert C. Liden, "Effects of Impression Management on Performance Ratings: A Longitudinal Study," *Academy of Management Journal* 38, no. 1 (1995): 232. Much of what follows in this section is a synopsis of the literature review and empirical findings of this study.

# Epilogue

# THE RETIREMENT DINNER REVISITED

You may not recognize the author's name, but you'll surely recognize the phrase he coined. Long ago, Charles Sheldon penned a story about a fictitious congregation that was challenged by its pastor to ask, in the face of every situation, "What would Jesus do?" They took him up on the challenge and experienced remarkable and exciting changes in their lives.

Now, a century later, Sheldon's book, *In His Steps: What Would Jesus Do?* remains on Christian best-seller lists. More than that, as most readers of Christian books know, variations on Sheldon's question are published every year. Songwriters also adopt the theme and climb the pop charts on its insight. Bible study curricula use the theme as their centerpiece. Sermon series on the topic are too prevalent to count. And in perhaps the best evidence of the question's capacity to penetrate hearts, we see a growing number of teenagers wearing *WWJD* bracelets as reminders of what to consider in the heat of the moment. Some teens have even gone so far as to get a *WWJD* tattoo (in case they misplace the bracelet, I guess).

Clearly, Sheldon articulated a timeless phrase. He captured the essence of our calling with four words—with one question. Regardless of one's generation, for those who desire to be Christlike, answering *"WWJD?"* is the first step. And in this book, I have made the assumption that the Beatitudes provide a timeless answer to that question. What would Jesus do in today's workplace? He would live by the Beatitudes.

There is a second step, though. It won't ever become a tattoo or a bumper sticker or a song, but it is a step that is, for the serious Christian, no less important than the first. After we ask, "What would Jesus do?" our calling is then to put our answer into practice—that is, to *do what Jesus would do.* Not exactly and easy task because, as I've argued throughout this book, in most cases to *do* what Jesus would do will require overcoming something that stands in your way. In your work life, it could be a golden calf: pride, career success, big bucks, popularity, people-pleasing. Or the primary obstacle for you could be a despised job. Some days it could be a misconception about meekness or rights. It could be compassion fatigue, ingratitude, or a penchant for payback. Whatever it is, every challenge to living your faith in the workplace calls for you to do more than look at a bracelet and ask a question. God wants you to move from asking to doing—to identify the major obstacles that stand between your current work life and His will for your work life—and to defeat those obstacles one day at a time.

OK, I'll be the first to say it: *DWJWD* will never make it in the world of wrist-fashion (notwithstanding its chic symmetry). It does remind us, though, of how easy it is to stall after the asking stage. And when we do stall after this first step, it's a real tragedy since our *behavior* is our best witness, not our knowledge of right and wrong. "Do not merely listen to the word, and so deceive yourself. Do what it says" (James 1:22). This is a verse that many learned way back in Sunday school for this very reason. It's bedrock. It's foundational. Being Christlike means *being* like Christ. That's how others will measure the value of your faith.

Think of it this way. If I were to inquire of your co-workers or your neighbors about your Christian character, nine out of ten of them won't point to your ability to answer theological questions or your brilliant arguments in defense of the gospel. No, those nine will cite your day-to-day actions, your behaviors, and your attitudes. Did you walk that lofty talk, or did they find the hypocrisy that many of them were looking to find all along?

Therefore, we have to take that second step—to *DWJWD*. To help you with that transition from asking to doing, then, allow me to make one general observation about overcoming whatever obstacles stand in your way.

If you're reading this chapter last (unlike what I often do since I like to see where a nonfiction book is going), you've probably deduced something striking about the obstacles to Christlikeness: The vast majority of them are *internal issues*. That is, they reside inside of us. Indeed, some obstacles to Christlikeness are external—a function of circumstances (like a lousy job, an oppressive boss, or a hostile work cul-

ture). But look at most of the others we've covered—
things like pride, greed, aggressiveness, a rights-
focused mind-set, fatigue, ingratitude, revenge, and
the desire to please people. They're internal. And because they're internal, I have some good news to report. You can start addressing these obstacles this
very day—*unilaterally.* Nothing else in your work life
has to change first. You don't have to quit your job,
change your circumstances, or pack your bags and go
to seminary. Instead, the enduring, biblically based
solution is to change your basic orientation to the
work you do, to the people around you on the job,
and to your entire career. Address the internal problems by changing the way you think. Reevaluate and
adjust your priorities. Align your view of *why you
work* and *what matters at work* to match God's view.

---

*The solution is to change your
basic orientation to your work,
to the people around you on the
job, and to your entire career.*

---

This is one of the most profound teachings in the
New Testament. It genuinely has the power to change
your life. Paul, I think, summarized it best in his classic verse: "Do not conform any longer to the pattern
of this world, but be transformed by the renewing of
your mind" (Romans 12:2).

The renewing of your mind. It's an internal solution to internal obstacles. The most critical battle is not external to you. It's not beyond your control. It doesn't require anyone else to change first. If you want to be more Christlike in your job and everywhere else, the most critical battle is within. Discipline yourself to fight this battle every day. That fight is a large part of what it means to be a committed Christian and to stay the course.

Please don't let that just splash off your back. Take a moment, if you would, to reflect on the likely consequences of your victory. They're really pretty extraordinary. Think about just how much more meaningful your work would seem if you fought that battle authentically. Think about how many lives you could impact by taking seriously the "renewing of your mind," the realignment of your workplace mindset, *the reconceptualization of your job as a ministry.*

---

*The most critical battle is within.*

---

In fact, to see these likely outcomes more clearly, take these last two minutes to return full circle to the point where our journey began in this book. Remember the room? Remember the occasion, your retirement dinner? Remember the underdressed party crasher now holding the microphone? Imagine for a moment that you actually took His advice today—that you sought to win this internal battle and to

adopt His definition of what matters most on the job.
Imagine that you decided to pursue "success" only in
the eyes of God throughout your career. Decades after that pivotal day of decision, what would that Man
with the microphone say? Perhaps something like this?

---

"I want to tell you what this person did on the job
that I think *really mattered.* Years ago, he turned
everything around by making a decision—the decision to dedicate all of his work to God. Everything he
did. Every project he undertook. Every screw he
turned. Every client he served. Everything. Did you
ever wonder why his work ethic has become legendary around here? Ever wonder how he was able to
pursue even the little stuff with such energy? It's because he's what I'd call 'poor in spirit,' working with
all of his heart as working for the Lord, not for men.
Let me tell you, *that* matters.

"His decision also led him to be gentle with people—co-workers, subordinates, customers, suppli-
ers—everyone. I'll be honest with you; it wasn't really
in his nature, but he overcame that. When people
pushed his buttons, he learned to handle the conflict
with Christian maturity. Gently. Emotionally con-
trolled. When people disagreed with his solutions, he
remained calm. Respectful. A charitable listener and
a willing collaborator. That's typical of My servant.
He's meek in the best sense of the word. *That* matters.

"Some of you were around when the firm imple-
mented that new customer-service system—right?
Everyone knows that it's done wonders for this organi-

zation. What no one knows, though, is that the idea was conceived by someone who was then a low-level employee—the man sitting in this chair next to Me. You didn't know that, did you? You thought it was that clever guy Jacob, who left the firm a few years back, right? That's because when My servant's idea was stolen from him, he let it go. Never said a word about it. Sure he could've claimed what was rightfully his, but My Father prompted him not to. The other guy needed the career boost, so My servant here put his rights on the shelf. The man is passionately God centered. And *that* matters.

"He's passionate about mercy too. He really cares about people. Year after year, he led the Toys for Tots campaign at this firm. Year after year, he hired people who were otherwise considered unemployable— gave them a second chance in life. Louie, you're one of them. Marie, you're another. Look at you now! Self-sufficient and raising families in homes of your own. Beyond that, My servant always made time to listen when somebody had a problem. He never seemed too busy for it, did he? Even gave you money out of his own pocket when he had some. Let Me ask you: How many of your lives were personally touched by this person's caring attitude?" At least three dozen hands go up around the room. "Tell Me something: Do those hands matter?

"And how 'bout this? Can any of you ever remember this guy complaining when things weren't going quite right? Anyone? That's because he never did. Not even that time he got laid off. Not even during that recession when nobody got a pay raise for two years straight. Instead, he made a habit of being thankful for what he *did* have in life. Made him the happiest guy around. It kept him what I'd call 'pure in heart.' Folks, *that* matters.

"Let Me close with this, My friends. I know that a few of you have been a little put off because My friend here is a Christian. Some of you have even given him a hard time about it throughout the years. A person like this doesn't always fit. And because of that reality, some of My other brothers and sisters have yielded to the pressure—saved their reputation at the expense of their faith. But this brother never did. Not once. He didn't get into anybody's face over those incidents, either. He never got even or caused a fuss. Never thought in terms of an 'eye for an eye.' Instead, he forgave you and used that hardship to become *stronger.* It helped him to work for God all the more! Ultimately, it helped him to serve your needs all the better. It gave him the opportunity to show you that being a believer will see you through life's trials. And you know what? As a result, some of those persecutors eventually became friends of Mine! That matters—*a lot.*

"It's true, this guy never made vice president and never earned an impressive paycheck, but in My Book, *he had the most successful of careers.* Just look around the room for a moment . . . his *real* success is measured in tears. He impacted your lives with his character, with his generosity, with his compassion—indeed, with his love for you. He discovered decades ago what I invite each of you to discover tonight: *What matters most in the workplace is the extent to which you are Christlike.* I tell you truly, My friends, nothing else even comes close.

"Well done, My good and faithful servant!"